Los Angeles to San Diego

Mls.		STATIONS	†No. 70 Daily	No. 72 Daily	†No. 74 Daily	No. 76 Daily	No. 10 Daily	No. 54 Daily	
			AM	AM	PM	PM	AM	PM	
0	Lv	Los Angeles	7.40	9.15	**5.00**	**9.00**	8.00	x **5.20**	
2		Redondo Junction						f **5.24**	
3		Hobart						f **5.28**	
7		Bandini						f **5.30**	
10		Rivera				f **9.18**		f **5.33**	
12		Los Nietos				f **9.21**		f **5.36**	
13		Santa Fe Springs	SAN DIEGAN		SAN DIEGAN			**5.39**	
17		La Mirada				f **9.21**		f **5.46**	
19		Buena Park				f **9.31**		f **5.52**	
23		Fullerton		9 50		**9.40**	8.33	**6.02**	
26		Anaheim		9.56		**9.44**			
31		Orange		10.04		**9.52**			
34		Santa Ana	8.20	10.10	**5.40**	**10 02**			
37		Venta							
41		Irvine		f10.22		f**10.12**			
46		El Toro		f10.29		f**10.20**			
50		Galivan							
56		S. J. Capistrano		f10.42		f**10.32**			
58		Serra (Doheny Park)				f**10.37**			
62		San Clemente		f10.51		f**10.43**			
67		San Onofre		f10.59		f**10.50**			
72		Agra							
77		Las Flores							
80		Stuart				f**11.08**			
85		Oceanside	9.17	11.30	**6.37**	**11.20**			
88		Carlsbad				f**11.25**			
92		Ponto							
95		Leucadia							
96		Encinitas		f11.48		f**11.40**			
98		Cardiff				f**11.42**			
101		Solana Beach				f**11.45**			
102		Del Mar		f11.55		f**11.50**			
107		Sorrento				f**11.58**			
111		Linda Vista				f12.08			
113		Selwyn							
115		Elvira							
118		Ladrillo				f12.17			
126	Ar	San Diego	10.10	**12.30**	**7.30**	f12.30			

Parlor cars are run on trains 70, 72, 74 and 76, Los Angeles to San Diego, and on 71, 73, 75 and 77, San Diego to Los Angeles.

16 Section Air-conditioned Tourist car and Air-conditioned Reclining Chair car San Diego to Chicago on No. 75 to Los Angeles, No. 2, The Scout, to Chicago, and on No. 72 Los Angeles to San Diego, from Chicago on No. 1, The Scout.

8 Sec. Comp. D. R. car (Air-Conditioned) San Diego to Chicago on No. 75 to Los Angeles, No. 4, the California Limited, to Chicago, and on No. 72 Los Angeles to San Diego, from Chicago on No. 3, the California Limited.

No. 71 will stop at any station to pick up revenue passengers destined to points east or north of Barstow, also to points Santa Barbara or north. Nos. 72 and 76 will stop at any station to discharge revenue passengers from points east or north of Barstow or from points, Santa Barbara or north. No. 72 will stop on flag at Los Nietos and La Mirada to pick up revenue passengers destined to San Diego. No. 75 will stop at Los Nietos and La Mirada to discharge revenue passengers from San Diego.

Nos. 72 and 76 will stop at Carlsbad to discharge revenue passengers from Los Angeles.

† All seats on the San Diegan, both parlor car and coach, are reserved. × Motor. f Stops on flag only.

San Diego to Los Angeles

Mls.		STATIONS	No. 71 Daily	†No. 73 Daily	No. 75 Daily	†No. 77 Daily	No 51 Daily	No. 53 Daily		
			AM	AM	PM	PM	AM	PM		
0	Lv	San Diego	8.15	10.50	**3.00**	**8.15**				
8		Ladrillo								
11		Elvira								
15		Linda Vista								
19		Sorrento								
24		Del Mar	f 8.48		**3.33**					
26		Solana Beach			f **3.36**					
28		Cardiff		SAN DIEGAN		SAN DIEGAN				
30		Encinitas	f 8.56		f **3.41**					
31		Leucadia								
34		Ponto								
38		Carlsbad	f 9.07		f **3.52**					
41		Oceanside	9.17	11.43	**4.05**	**9.07**				
44		Stuart								
49		Las Flores								
54		Agra								
59		San Onofre			f **4.27**					
64		San Clemente	f 9.41		f **4.33**					
68		Serra (Doheny Pk)								
70		S. J. Capistrano	f 9.49		**4.43**					
76		Galivan								
80		El Toro	f10.02		f **4.56**					
85		Irvine			f **5.03**					
92		Santa Ana	10.20	**12.37**	**5.16**	**10.02**				
95		Orange	10.25		**5.21**			x **2.47**		
100		Anaheim	10.31		**5.30**			**2.57**		
103		Fullerton	10.36		**5.37**		x 8.23	**3.05**		
107		Buena Park					f 8.32	f **3.12**		
109		La Mirada					f 8.35	f **3.16**		
113		Santa Fe Springs					f 8.41	f **3.22**		
114		Los Nietos					f 8.44	f **3.25**		
116		Rivera					f 8.49	f **3.29**		
119		Bandini						f **3.33**		
123		Hobart					f 8.57	f **3.37**		
124		Redondo Jct						f **3.40**		
126	Ar	Los Angeles	11.15	**1.20**	**6.15**	**10 45**	9.10	**3.55**		

f Flag stop. × Motor.

Grand Canyon

Read Down — Read Up

No.14	‡AUTO STAGE	‡AUTO STAGE	‡AUTO STAGE	Mls.	STATIONS	No.15	‡AUTO STAGE	‡AUTO STAGE	‡AUTO STAGE
AM	PM	AM	AM			PM	AM	PM	PM
4.20	**6.30**	11.00	7.30	0	Lv . . Williams . . . Ar	**11.05**	10.45	**12.15**	**4.15**
6.45	**8.15**	**12.45**	9.15	64	Ar . Grand Canyon Lv	**8.45**	9.00	10.30	**2.30**

‡Tickets reading via rail between Williams and Grand Canyon will be exchanged for stage tickets by agents at Williams or Grand Canyon without additional collection.

Yosemite Valley Service

Santa Fe to Merced, thence Yosemite Valley R. R. and Auto

Mls.		STATIONS	No. 110-10		Mls.		STATIONS	No. 9-109	
			PM					PM	
0	Lv	San Francisco	**11.00**		0	Lv	Yosemite (Auto)	**12.50**	
9		Oakland	**11.40**		15	Lv	El Portal (Y.V.R.R.)	**1.45**	
88		Stockton	1.58		92	Ar	Merced	**5.10**	
153	Ar	Merced	3.38		92	Lv	Merced (S.F. Station)	* **1.35**	
150	Lv	Merced (Y.V.R.R.)	* 8.15		157	Ar	Stockton	3.25	
227	Ar	El Portal	11.40		236	Ar	Oakland	6.05	
242	Ar	Yosemite (Auto)	**12 40**		242	Ar	San Francisco	6.30	

Mls.		STATIONS	No. 9		Mls.		STATIONS	No. 10	
0	Lv	Bakersfield	**9.10**		0	Lv	Yosemite (Auto)	**12.50**	
80		Hanford	**10.52**		15		El Portal (Y.V.R.R.)	**1.45**	
110		Fresno	12 05		92	Ar	Merced	**5.10**	
168	Ar	Merced	1.35		92	Lv	Merced (S.F. Station)	* **3.38**	
168	Lv	Merced (Y.V.R.R.)	* 8.15		150	Ar	Fresno	4.55	
245	Ar	El Portal	11.40		190	Ar	Hanford	6.08	
260	Ar	Yosemite (Auto)	**12.40**		260	Ar	Bakersfield	7.55	

*Connecting Train.

Santa Fe-Yosemite Transportation System

Read down — Santa Fe to Merced thence Yosemite Transportation System — Read up

			STATIONS			
			Lv . . . . . . San Francisco . . . . . . Ar			
			. . . . Oakland			
			Ar . . . . . . Merced S. Fe Lv			
			Lv (Auto) Merced Y. T. S. (Auto) Ar			
			Ar . . . . Yosemite Lv			
			STATIONS			
			Lv . . . . . . Bakersfield . . . . . . Ar			
			. . . . Hanford			
			. . . . Fresno . . . . Ar			
			Ar . . . . . . Merced S. Fe Lv			
			Lv . . . (Auto) Merced (Auto) . . Ar			
			Ar . . . . . Yosemite Y. T. S Lv			

reasons why you should ride the train between

LOS ANGELES & SAN DIEGO

- *Economy*: Very low round trip and one way fares.
- *Speed*: Now trains as fast as two and a half hours each way.
- *Safety*: Automatic block signals—alert train crews.
- *Comfort*: Big roomy coaches—dustless and joltless.
- *Convenience*: Four daily "on time" trains each way.
- *Scenic*: Along the ocean—thru verdant orange groves.

The Surfliners

SIGNOR
'85

The Surfliners

50 years of

by Dick Stephenson

TRANS-ANGLO BOOKS • Glendale, California

Front Cover

San Diegan No. 577 slips along the shoreline just south of Del Mar on August 27, 1988. The train is powered by F40 No. 222, while cab car No. 9637 graces the rear. **Dick Stephenson**

Back Cover

Top: *On the first day of service under Amtrak, No. 77 crests the grade at Miramar behind F7 No. 342.* **John E. Shaw**

Bottom: *Despite a population and building explosion in Orange County, Valencia has retained a country flavor. Here, No. 72 blasts through Valencia in July 1985. The Irvine Country Store has been preserved, and moved to a new site.* **Jim Minor**

Inside Front Cover

*Left: The initial **San Diegan** promotion from March 1938 includes some eye-catching graphics to underscore the 2½ hour schedule and new equipment. Right: The March 27, 1938, schedules include the new streamlined **San Diegan** as well as other passenger services.* **Brian Norden Collection**

Inside Back Cover

Left: This 1938 map details Santa Fe's lines in California, and include some location names no longer used. Right: Santa Fe proudly introduced a number of new trainsets in 1938, as this promotional cut shows. **Brian Norden Collection**

Frontispiece

*"Orange County Memories," an original oil painting by artist John R. Signor, depicts the passage of **San Diegan** No. 74 through the undeveloped lands of the Irvine Ranch in 1962. Alco PA set No. 51 L, A, C, reengined with EMD prime movers, powers the train through the orange groves in the shadow of Santiago Peak, better known as Saddleback Mountain.*

Contents Page

***San Diegan** No. 75 crosses the Los Angeles River near Redondo Junction in the summer of 1969. Two units were typical for non-peak trains.* **Dick Stephenson**

THE SURFLINERS

ISBN 87046-084-6

Published by TRANS-ANGLO BOOKS, a division of INTERURBAN PRESS
P.O. Box 6444 • Glendale, California 91205

Printed and bound in the United States of America

FOREWORD

WHILE THE OVERALL history of the Los Angeles to San Diego Surf Line goes back 100 years, the emphasis of this book is on the years since 1938.

That is why, in the first chapter, we briefly deal with the first connections of San Diego to the outside (railwise) world. Over the years many things have changed. The various on-line cities have developed, grown and multiplied, and grown again. Where much of the area used to be open fields, there now is virtually solid development all along the way except through Camp Pendleton (San Onofre to Oceanside).

The San Diego Corridor, as it is now called, has attracted national attention. Here, in an area where the automobile is revered, if not worshipped, intrastate rail passenger service has established an important toehold. With state and local governmental support it seems that drivers are finally considering the train as an alternative to driving. This is a good omen for corridors in other areas.

Geography, sociology and politics all play a part in these developments, and there certainly has been the right combination of factors on the Surf Line.

While the trains that run on the line and the people who run them have changed considerably over the years, the trains still run to the same places, even if now for new reasons.

Come with us now as we look at fifty years of *San Diegan* service in words and pictures.

—DICK STEPHENSON

SEPTEMBER 1988

ACKNOWLEDGEMENTS

THE AUTHOR WISHES to acknowledge the generous contributions of time and effort by many persons connected with the project, especially Clifford R. Prather, Greg Luiz, Jim Minor, Rick Peterson and Jim Walker. Without their assistance the completion of this project would have been nearly impossible.

Thanks are also extended to Mike Blaszak, Bob Kern, Stan Kistler, Dennis Kogan, Ralph Melching, Brian Norden, Dennis Ryan, John Signor, Don Sims and Ed Von Nordeck.

A special word of thanks to my wife Martha for her effort and determination in proofreading the text, and to Paul Hammond for his expertise in the layout and appearance of the book.

We realize that every possible event and piece of equipment cannot be covered in a book of this scope, so it is planned for a second volume to be published in 1989 or 1990. Both color and black and white photos are being sought, especially of pre-1955 views. Submissions may be sent to the author in care of Interurban Press, P.O. Box 6444, Glendale, CA 91205. Photographers whose work is published will receive a complimentary copy of the book.

30
43
43
SANTA FE

Contents

38
SANTA FE
38

1

The Glory Years

RAIL SERVICE BETWEEN Los Angeles and San Diego was somewhat secondary to the establishment of through service to the East from San Diego. Given its natural harbor, it was a desirable terminus for a line, the California Southern Railway, which was completed to Colton after some difficulty in 1882. The completion of Santa Fe's line through Cajon Pass in November 1885 meant that strained cooperation with the Southern Pacific could revert to the fierce competition these two companies had enjoyed for many years.

The building of the line through Orange to Los Angeles and San Bernardino (via Santa Ana Canyon) was of secondary importance to the California Southern Railway. Construction took place in 1887 and 1888. The on-line cities of Santa Ana and San Juan Capistrano were not large then, but rich growing lands were tapped, and more importantly, two important connections were developed: through Santa Ana Canyon to San Bernardino and beyond, and to Los Angeles. Both of these connections provided outlets for freight and passengers to other communities (and even other carriers).

The Surf Line took on new importance when the original main line through Temecula Canyon washed out for the third time in 1891. Santa Fe decided not to rebuild the original line, so the Surf Line became the main route for goods and people to move to and from the growing port city of San Diego.

And grow it did, from a small settlement of a few thousand in the late 1800s to a metropolis of over one million in the mid-1980s. Two important Expositions helped put it on the map as well. The Panama-Pacific Exposition in 1915 ranks as one of the most important activities in the development of the city; many of the buildings in Balboa Park date from that event even if their use has changed over the years. The California Pacific International Exposition in 1935–36 brought many needed tourist dollars to the city during the Depression.

The majority of the rail travelers to these events were carried aboard cars of the Santa Fe. Service was comfortable and dependable, and the railway had certainly worked very hard to establish itself as a provider of quality service. Even if San Diego was not directly a part of the transcontinental route, there were still a number of traditions to be maintained—the San Diego service was viewed as an adjunct to long-distance service to the East. (More will be said about this in Chapter Two.)

By the mid-thirties Santa Fe had a well-established record for operating its trains to and from San Diego. On-line cities had grown and prospered by that time, and had even seen a minor and major conflict fought and won. Caught in the doldrums of the Depression as was every major carrier in the country, Santa Fe was faced with choices to make in terms of how to attract more travelers to its line. Union Pacific and Burlington led the way with fast,

*A classic view of a southbound **San Diegan** of the fifties finds four-unit F7 set No. 38 at San Clemente. The old depot is visible behind the train.* **Santa Fe Railway**

economical streamliners, and Southern Pacific made quite a splash in 1937 with the introduction of its colorful *Coast Daylight* streamliner (though improvements on SP long-haul trains were still a few years away). Santa Fe was not about to be outdone by the roads it competed with for long-distance business.

Starting with the remarkable lightweight *Super Chief* which entered service in May 1937, Santa Fe made a major commitment to upgrading and reequipping its passenger fleet. It was more than merely an adman's pitch to say that "1938 was a Santa Fe year." In a major blitz, twelve new trainsets were introduced in a four-month period. These included a second trainset for the *Super Chief* (permitting twice-weekly service), six sets for the *Chief,* two sets for the *El Capitan* (also twice-weekly on the same fast 39¾ hour schedule used by the *Super Chief),* two sets for the *Kansas Cityan* and *Chicagoan,* and last, but not least, one set for the *San Diegan.* Here was what Santa Fe proudly referred to as ". . . the most numerous and varied array of ultra-modern passenger equipment possessed by any American railroad."

Coach Fare Amenities

Probably the most significant trend to come out of the equipment upgrading of the thirties was the extension of luxury amenities much more broadly to coach fare passengers. For years there had been many improvements and upgradings made for the benefit of first-class travelers. Before the Depression, services such as lounge, barber, bath and valet were provided for first-class passengers. Those who could not afford at least tourist sleeping-car accommodations frequently found themselves riding long distances in non-air conditioned coaches with hard seats, maybe packing their own food with them for the trip. It comes as no surprise then that this new equipment which brought many of the modern conveniences right down to the coach passenger, and often at excursion fares of less than a penny-a-mile, seemed like a dream come true. Passengers flocked to the new trains like ducks to water. The introduction of air conditioning just a few years earlier had been heralded as a major improvement, but it had nowhere near the impact of the lightweight equipment pulled by modern diesels on faster schedules.

•

This, then, provides some background to the period when the first lightweight *San Diegan* equipment was introduced in March of 1938. The cars and locomotives fit into the larger scheme of a major investment by the railway, and in a sense, guaranteed that luxurious modern equipment was available for the entire run from Chicago right to San Diego, with a quick change in Los Angeles.

Train No. 71 prepares to depart the brand-new San Diego depot in 1915, with engine No. 1273 heading up a seven-car consist of heavyweights and an older wood-bodied car. Rail photography at the depot hasn't changed much over the years, as this view shows.
R.P. Middlebrook/Bob Kern Collection

Above: A large crowd was on hand at San Diego to welcome the first regularly scheduled ***San Diegan*** *(train No. 1-70) on March 27, 1938. Unit No. 7 and her consist started a long tradition that continues today. Below: For almost 14 months,* ***San Diegans*** *operated from La Grande Station in Los Angeles. Looking north, E1 No. 7 and consist represent No. 70, while No. 72 is seen two tracks to the right.* **Both photos, Ralph Melching**

*Right: Speeding northbound through San Clemente on July 17, 1937, the spruced-up equipment from the **Valley Flyer** was used on runs to San Diego even before the lightweight **San Diegans** were introduced. The **Flyer** trainset also augmented the streamlined **San Diegans** into the early forties. Below: New four-unit FT set No. 100 leaves Los Angeles Union Passenger Terminal on a demonstration run to San Diego on February 12, 1941. The FTs were an important factor in the handling of wartime traffic.*

Gerald M. Best/ Bob Kern Collection; Phillips C. Kauke

An Immediate Hit

When the new equipment was introduced in 1938, the public was quick to accept it and give it hearty approval. The new train made two round trips per day between Los Angeles and San Diego, barely allowing the crews sufficient time to clean the windows and maintain the equipment.

On June 12, 1938, the schedules were changed, and trains 71, 74, 75 and 78 were designated as *San Diegans* on a fast two-hour 30-minute schedule. There were days when the diesel failed, however, so a variety of steamers filled in on these occasions.

Wartime Traffic Boom

With the introduction of the second set of streamlined *San Diegan* equipment on June 8, 1941, four of the five daily round trips were *San Diegans*. This hardly mattered, however, for soon World War II arrived and the line be-

Above: Climbing Miramar Hill with a troop train, 2-8-2 No. 3142, helps 4-8-2 No. 3737 to Linda Vista on May 11, 1943. This grade remains the most restrictive part of the Surf Line today. Below: World War II traffic strained the abilities of the line almost to the breaking point. "Mountain"-type No. 3739 drifts downgrade near Elvira on August 16, 1943, with a troop train which includes five ex-Interurban Electric Railway trailers.

R.P. Middlebrook/Bob Kern Collection; R.P. Middlebrook/Stan Kistler Collection

"Mountain"-type 3747 leads a troop train into San Diego in 1944. The ex-IER cars saw considerable service in moving troops during the war, as they were no longer needed in the Bay Area. **R.P. Middlebrook/Stan Kistler Collection**

Through Sleeper Service to San Diego

For years before the *San Diegan* trains were introduced, Santa Fe operated through Pullmans from the East to San Diego. Even during the Depression, a sleeper was operated to San Diego off the *California Limited* and often the *Chief.* After the *Scout* was added to the Santa Fe fleet to provide "luxurious economy travel," its service was extended by adding a through tourist sleeper and chair car to San Diego.

After the first *San Diegan* trainset was inaugurated in 1938 on the Surf Line, the through cars from the *Scout* and the *California Limited* were operated on one of the remaining conventional trains. In late 1938 the car from the *California Limited* was eliminated; the cars from the *Scout* were dropped June 2, 1940. During the war and up to 1947, there was no through service, and connections were made in Los Angeles.

When through service resumed, it was with a lightweight car of the 8 section–2 compartment–2 drawing room configuration. This car operated east in the *Chief* after being switched from No. 71. Westbound, the car was added to No. 74.

In the spring of 1951 the through sleeper became a transcontinental car to Washington, D.C. (a natural for military and related travel), and the assigned equipment was *Valley*-series 6 section–6 roomette–4 double bedroom cars. From Chicago the car was handled in the B&O's *Capitol Limited* eastbound and on the *Shenandoah* westbound, connecting with the *Chief.* In the fall of 1951 the equipment was changed to a 10 roomette–6 double bedroom car. When the assigned cars were shopped, the 8-2-2 cars were used in their place. Somewhat of an "orphan" to the rest of the fleet, these cars were valued in this service for their sections (upper and lower berths), because military travel requests were honored for sections (though roomettes were substituted when berths were not operated in a particular service).

In January 1954, the transcontinental sleepers were switched from the *Chief* to the *Super Chief.* With other operational changes made in June 1954, the service was discontinued.

The operation of the through sleeper had been another indication that the San Diego service was an adjunct of the mainline service, and had contributed a number of connecting passengers.

(Thanks to Brian Norden and Ed Von Nordeck for background on this service.)

came incredibly busy. Many extra sections and troop trains were operated, both from Los Angeles, and directly from the East through Atwood and Orange. To help meet the great increase in demand, 25 ex-Interurban Electric cars were used as coaches on the line during the war.

With major military installations directly served by the Surf Line, traffic swelled to levels that had never been imagined before the war. This glut of business, necessitating helpers for Miramar Hill in both directions, hastened the installation of Centralized Traffic Control as a means of improving the efficiency of the line. This installation was unique in that two machines controlled the line from Old Town in San Diego all the way up through Fullerton to D.T. Junction (near Rivera [later Pico Rivera]) on the Third District. This proved very helpful on the Fullerton-Los Angeles segment of the line which, in 1943, saw traffic density grow to about 100 movements per day including both passenger and freight. The control operators at Fullerton and Oceanside were not dispatchers, and although they controlled switches and signals, they needed the concurrence of the train dispatcher in San Bernardino to set up meets between trains.

After the war, the machines were moved to San Bernardino and operated in a more conventional manner. In 1946, for example, even with CTC in effect, train order offices were still maintained at Fullerton, Santa Ana, San Juan Capistrano, Oceanside, Linda Vista and San Diego. This was, however, a reduction of ten offices from just two years earlier.

Postwar Boom

If there was any area of the country that took off and did well after the war, it was Southern California. With a moderate climate, plenty of land, and lots of job opportunities, it was a natural to do well. People had money in their pockets, and a yearning to spend it and go on pleasure trips which had been denied them by the constraints of the wartime period. *San Diegan* consists swelled to twelve and thirteen cars to accommodate the increase in business. As covered elsewhere, there was a through sleeper to/from Washington, D.C., plus lounge and dining service. This period of time can easily be described as the glory years, when paralleling highways were far from multi-lane Interstates, and jet aircraft were still in the future.

To improve the efficiency of the line, in 1946 some realignment work in Rose Canyon and at Ponto (near Leucadia) was undertaken. In 1948, double track was installed between Santa Ana and Venta (near Irvine), and the segment between Linda Vista and Elvira was tied together, eliminating Selwyn siding but giving a nearly five-mile stretch of double track in Rose Canyon that came in handy for meeting trains.

Service Peaks at Seven Trains

The postwar peak came with the introduction of two Budd-built rail diesel cars to *San Diegan* service on May

Brand-new RDC cars Nos. DC 191 and 192 attract considerable attention on their first day of regular service—May 21, 1952, as seen in front of the San Diego depot. **R.P. Middlebrook/Stan Kistler Collection**

Right: The RDCs are seen cruising south through the orange groves north of San Juan Capistrano in 1952. Many good things were expected of the lightweight, speedy Budd cars, but instead they left the area under a dark cloud following a tragic wreck in Los Angeles in January 1956. Below: Operating as train No. 83, the RDCs pause at Del Mar on November 13, 1955. On the other side of the station is No. 74 waiting in the siding to meet No. 83. One can date RDC photos by the number of modifications which had been made, such as painting of the ends (compare with photo above). **Stan Kistler; John Shaw**

A favorite of ***San Diegan*** *crews, 4-8-4 No. 2929 works upgrade northbound on Miramar Hill (near the top) in 1951, just two years before steam power was discontinued on the San Diego line.* **R.P. Middlebrook/Stan Kistler Collection**

21, 1952. With their introduction, there were four *San Diegan* runs each way daily, plus two RDC runs and one local (carrying mail and express, using older heavyweight cars, and making frequent stops). The RDCs operated morning and afternoon round trips as trains 70-71 and 82-83. Number 82 was a two-hour and 15-minute nonstop trip southbound, which met one train on the way. This sounds remarkable compared with today's schedules, but remember that there was a lot of open space along the line in those days . . . more crossings too, but a lot fewer opposing vehicles.

The RDCs did get their share of scrapes from grade-crossing accidents. One can just about date photos of the RDCs by how many modifications had been made, including the repainting of the ends of both cars to red with the yellow oval Santa Fe emblem; they made a few trips to San Bernardino Shops for patch-up work. When out of the lineup, they were replaced by a single PA and a handful of coaches, which could not quite equal the fast running time of the RDCs. On rare instances just one of the RDCs was used by itself.

End of An Era

Between the growing fleet of diesels and the RDC cars, steam on the San Diego line was relegated to less and less of a role. In general, it was being phased down or out throughout the region by 1951. Second sections, Del Mar Race specials and Korean War troop trains were still perfect reasons for the use of reliable 4-8-4s of the 2900, 3751 and 3776 classes, however. In 1953 the final chapter of steam power was written when two additional sets of three-unit, dual-service F7s were purchased, and delivered in May. The 339 and 340 F7 sets became the spare passenger units assigned to the Los Angeles Division, and thereby spelled the end of steam. By 1953 the only remaining line-side service was water at Oceanside, and all steam-powered trains stopped there in either direction for a drink.

Mention should also be made of 4-8-4 2929, which was a regular on the Los Angeles Division from the late forties onward. When other members of that modern class of steam were productively employed in the Midwest, 2929

Station switchers at San Diego were frequently Alco S2s, such as No. 2363 seen here on November 29, 1952, at the north end of the depot. **John Shaw**

Two "Spot Class" motors, E1 Nos. 5 and 3, lay over at San Diego on April 24, 1946. Side panel work on No. 5 was completed later that year. Below: Freshly returned from rebuilding at EMD, E8m No. 83 poses at San Diego on March 7, 1953. Below right: E8m No. 81 and a mate pass Mission Tower as they return to Redondo Jct. Roundhouse after bringing No. 73 to Los Angeles in July 1953.
Top and below, R.P. Middlebrook/Stan Kistler Collection; below right, Elmer K. Hall

was rolling to and from San Diego on an almost daily basis. She was a good steamer and well liked by the crews.

The end of steam came finally on August 23, 1953, when class engine 3751 pulled Nos. 72-73.

Stalwart E Units

This chapter would not be complete without a salute to the "Spot Class" E1s (2-9). These sleek, slant-nosed passenger cab units were akin to the Founding Fathers of Dieseldom . . . the guys who were there when it all started. Originally delivered with 1,800-hp Winton engines, they were upgraded and modernized as time went by (between their delivery in 1938 and 1953, when they were returned to Electro-Motive for upgrading to E8 standards). The re-

*At left: Santa Fe's one set of Fairbanks-Morse cab units, Nos. 90L/A/B, are seen at San Diego on February 16, 1949. Below right: Mail train No. 75 (the last non-**San Diegan**) with nearly new F7 Nos. 335L/A/B pauses at San Juan Capistrano on July 23, 1953. The southbound mail train was a night job. Bottom: GP7 No. 2693 leads the supply train as it passes through Stuart (near Oceanside), also on July 23, 1953.*

Left: R.P. Middlebrook/ Stan Kistler Collection; Others: John Shaw

markable part is that they performed long and faithfully, running off hundreds of thousands of miles in *San Diegan* and other passenger service along the Santa Fe Trail. When rebuilt at EMD in 1953 they were given a new lease on life, so to speak. They returned to service as Nos. 80-87, and continued to run until the last of the class was retired in 1970. This was a remarkable record of service on anyone's railroad!

Footnote

To capture the flavor of what an average day on the Surf Line was like during the Glory Years, here are some notes on motive power and train size from Friday, August 15, 1947, as taken from the dispatcher's trainsheet.

Eastbound			Westbound		
Train	Power	Cars	Train	Power	Cars
70	3443	6	71	8-5	13
1-72	7-3A	12	73	7-3A	11
2-72	3747/3739	13[1]	75	3443	5
74	8-5	13	77	8-5	12
76	7-3A	12	Extra	3747/3739	13[1]
78	8-5	11	79	7-3A	13
SDX	3863	40-0[3]	SBX	3890	14-16
136	3894	48-0[3]	Extra	1821	11-24[2]
			135	3893	9-21[3]

Notes
1. Del Mar Race Special.
2. San Diego to Santa Ana.
3. Used engine 3856 as helper on Miramar Hill.

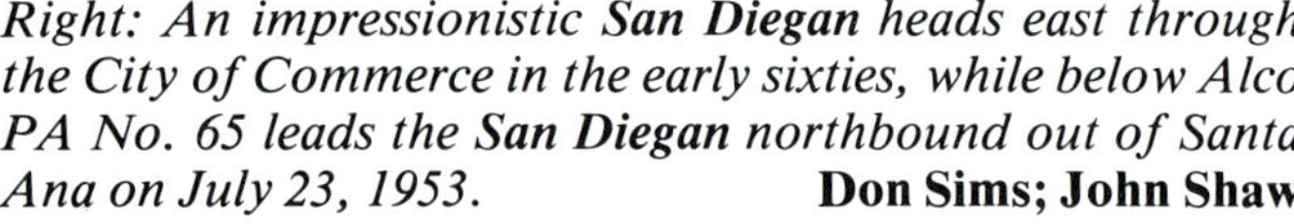

Right: An impressionistic **San Diegan** *heads east through the City of Commerce in the early sixties, while below Alco PA No. 65 leads the* **San Diegan** *northbound out of Santa Ana on July 23, 1953.* **Don Sims; John Shaw**

Idling the night away, locomotive 51L/A/C spends one of many nights of her long career in San Diegan service laying over at San Diego in this undated shot from the sixties. **John Sjolander Collection**

The "Christine" Saga

It is doubtful that anyone would intentionally set out to name a locomotive "Christine," but Santa Fe had a three-unit set of PAs that acquired that moniker.

When locomotive 51L-A-C emerged from the shops in 1955 with 1,750-hp EMD prime movers in each Alco-built body, the comparison to the first transsexual, Christine Jorgensen, was inevitable. It looked like one thing on the outside, but was something else on the inside. From a side view, the locomotive had a characteristic bulge in the roofline to accommodate the revision in mechanical equipment.

While the rebuilt unit had the reliability of the EMD powerplants, and the great ride of the Alco PAs, it just didn't have the pulling power of the true Alcos. Crews complained that the 51 trio was so underpowered it was approximately equivalent to two PAs. Roundhouse foremen, being the wise men that they were, would try to hold the 51 for secondary use such as race trains or specials, and in the sixties the 51L or 51C would be paired up with a regular PA (not so remarkable, as they were electrically compatible).

The 51 set was reduced by one cab unit when, on December 22, 1965, the 51C and 61 collided with a loaded gravel truck in Anaheim (near what is today Anaheim Stadium), with serious results. The two units turned over, the five-car train was derailed, the engine crew and some of the passengers were injured and the driver of the truck was killed. The two units were removed to San Bernardino and later scrapped (after being traded in to EMD in 1966).

The story does not end here, however, as the 51A was used in long-haul service thereafter until retired and traded in to EMD in 1968.

The 51L got the last laugh in this story, however, when electricians discovered that some of the electrical connections had never been wired correctly. This fixed, she was a considerably faster unit and could keep up with the best of them. She was retired in 1968 and traded in to EMD. By then, with passenger trains being discontinued and the passenger power pool shrinking, even the remaining "wolf in sheep's clothing" was excess, and no longer needed.

(Thanks to Cliff Prather and the late George Oliver for background information.)

252

2

Decline and Rebirth

IN TERMS OF DECLINING ridership and service reductions, the die had probably already been cast as to the fate of the *San Diegans* even before the tragic derailment of the RDC cars on January 22, 1956 (though some reports indicate there had been thoughts of expanding RDC service, as the cars were good performers with reasonable operating costs). The deaths of 30 passengers and injuries to 174 others in that accident left an indelible mark on the service. The RDCs were quietly replaced with a single PA and four cars, and sat in the Redondo Junction Roundhouse for a few months, eventually leaving the area to be rebuilt and reassigned to the Newton-to-Dodge City, Kansas, run. (They were pending disposition by 1968.)

Frequency Reductions

On April 28, 1956, the last heavyweight (non-*San Diegan)* locals, trains 70 and 75 were discontinued, reducing the service level to six trains each way per day. This level lasted only 18 months until October 28, 1957, when service was reduced to five daily trains with an extra weekend-only train. The discontinuance also meant that a number of small flagstop stations no longer had any regular passenger service.

Number 75 heads downgrade at MP 252 on Miramar Hill on September 5, 1967. Included in the consist are an SP horse express car (due to the end of the Del Mar racing season) and two baggage cars. **Rick Peterson**

This level of service was retained until July 31, 1964, when trains 70 and 81 were discontinued. The mail contract had not been renewed on July 1, 1964, and that business departed to be hauled by trucks.

While the 1964 discontinuance was not particularly opposed, Santa Fe's 1965 effort to drop another pair of trains, and weekend-only trains 79-80, brought about (for those days) a fair amount of opposition from passengers and others. A number of witnesses testified before the California Public Utilities Commission, especially regarding the loss of train 71, which had built up a commuter ridership (and probably was years ahead of its time). The Commission granted the discontinuances, however, and effective September 29, 1965, a three-trains-each-way-per-day frequency was reached. This level remained in place to the end of Santa Fe-operated service in 1971. Train numbers were 74, 76 and 78 and 73, 75 and 77.

Dependable Service

What typified the day-in-and-day-out operations of the sixties was the sameness. The trains ran, rain or shine, winter or summer. The backbone of the service was the Alco PA . . . so common that some fans almost lost interest in seeing the same motive power time after time. The cars were the same, the schedules were the same, only the people changed.

Looking forlorn and the worse for wear following the tragic accident, RDC Nos. 191 and 192 sit inside the Redondo Jct. Roundhouse on February 2, 1956. The cars were later rebuilt and reassigned to the Midwest.
Jim Walker

Left: Typical power for ***San Diegans*** *of the sixties, PA set No. 51 lays over at San Diego alongside a set of equipment on the hot night of July 6, 1959. Above: A very dated shot shows a northbound* ***San Diegan*** *making its station stop at Pico Rivera in the early sixties. Note the combination mail/baggage car.* **Henry J. Luna; Don Sims**

By the late sixties, however, things did change. A whole new generation of train riders descended upon the *San Diegans*. Weekend consists in the summers of 1968–70 swelled to 22 cars, and the kids became so unruly that railroad police had to ride the trains. San Clemente was the common destination, and even with gas at 28 cents a gallon the train took many youngsters right to the beach . . . and there were no parking tickets. "Groovy," said the kids; "Ouch!" said the Santa Fe, and even considered dropping the San Clemente stop in 1970 to lessen the problems. With only some trains stopping at San Clemente, the problem has moderated over the years. Today there is another generation of seasonal riders who like the convenience of the San Clemente stop.

Motive Power Changes

The Alco PAs became a staple item on *San Diegans* in the late fifties. They were supplemented by F units, especially on Del Mar Race Specials and other extra trains. By 1967, the PAs were rapidly getting tired. New passenger power was bought: FP45s 100-108, U28CGs 350-359 and U30CGs 400-405. The two latter models came from GE in 1966–67. They worked the *Grand Canyon,* and were used on *San Diegans* between September 1968 and February 1969. After a derailment at speed in Illinois on the *Grand Canyon,* they were temporarily withdrawn from service before being reassigned to the *Texas Chief*. All were even-

Located five air miles east of Fullerton, Olive is the principal city on the 5.8-mile Olive District. Though passenger service was discontinued years before, a rerouted ***San Diegan*** *(probably No. 76) heads south through Olive in the early sixties behind PA No. 61.*

Both photos, Ed Workman/ John Signor Collection

Above: A northbound ***San Diegan*** *glides past the depot in Orange in 1960 with "Christine" set No. 51 providing the power (see page 23 for more about "Christine"). Right: PA No. 61L and a sister lead a Del Mar Race Special as it pauses at Santa Ana. In the background is the SP-AT&SF interchange track.* **John Signor Collection**

Above: PA No. 67 leads a southbound train at Miramar in 1966. Reliability problems caused the PAs to more frequently be run in pairs. Right: No. 71 northbound from San Diego on Mondays brought back the power from Sunday-only train No. 80. Here at Morena siding near Mission Bay, four units easily handle the early morning train.

Dennis Kogan; John Sjolander Collection

Above: RS1 No. 2394 was long a fixture in San Diego, as seen here at 22nd St. Yard in 1965. The early roadswitcher has been preserved at the California State Railroad Museum. Below: Detail of the coach yard tracks at San Diego can be seen in this April 1968 shot. By this time the PAs had been withdrawn from service, and F7s, such as No. 43C and an F7B, were in command.

John Shaw; Robert L. Hogan

tually regeared and reassigned to freight service. The FP45s survive today as Santa Fe 5990-5998.

The tried-and-true F7s stepped back in to handle *San Diegans* after the aforementioned derailment, and continued to serve until July 1973, when Amtrak's SDP40Fs became available. The monster 22-car weekend trains required five F units, often in the A-B-B-B-B configuration. More than one fireman felt he had walked all the way from San Diego to Los Angeles in keeping the steam generators all functioning, which was necessary to keep the cars' steam ejector air-conditioning systems working. This was no speedy run, either, since two stops were necessary at some stations, and performance was a bit sluggish. In comparison, the off-peak trains were much more responsive, and able to keep the schedule. When the F40s and Amfleet cars arrived, they provided a higher level of performance because of their light weight and ability to accelerate and brake rapidly.

The Amtrak Era

When the National Railroad Passenger Corporation took over the operation of the nation's passenger trains on May 1, 1971, it had no polished organization skilled at running a nationwide rail passenger system. What it had was a diverse group of ex-railroad and airline people who hoped that somehow they could hold things together long enough to see some positive things happen. That entire development in itself would fill another volume, and won't

Left: U28CG No. 354 leads No. 74 south at Ponto, south of Oceanside in the fall of 1968, as Santa Fe tried using newer power on the ***San Diegans.*** *Below: In a scene that looks more like New England than Southern California, train No. 76 with U30CG No. 405 in command has two Santa Fe Big Dome cars and cafe-observation 1509 on the rear for an excursion party as it crosses the San Luis Rey River bridge in Oceanside on October 20, 1968.*

Both photos, Rick Peterson

Above: No. 77 loads passengers at Oceanside in 1967. After boarding, they could enjoy a snack and drink in chair-lounge car 1399, pictured behind them. Below: The doorway of the Oceanside depot provides a frame for a ***San Diegan*** *in 1970. Following the opening of the new Oceanside Transportation Center in 1984, the Santa Fe depot was razed in 1988.*
Both photos, Rick Peterson

Above: Train No. 76 backs out of LAUPT at Mission Tower in December 1968. In just a few moments, the train will reverse direction and head southward along the Los Angeles River.

Above: Illustrative of how the rail line runs through the Los Angeles industrial area, No. 76 is beside the Los Angeles River, at the 6th St. bridge. Below: No. 74 heads south along the river behind F3 No. 29 and four companions. At left is First St. Yard, which by this point in 1969 was no longer active; the 4th St. bridge is in the background.

Left: No. 76 heads onto single track at Bandini before crossing the Rio Hondo River in December 1968. This area was double-tracked in 1970, and currently is being studied for triple tracking. Below: Speeding through Pico Rivera on Labor Day, 1969, No. 76 is led by dual-service F7 No. 329, complete with single tone "cow" horn. This area likewise is being studied for triple tracking.

Two pages, Dick Stephenson

Trains sometimes grew long in the summertime! F7 No. 306 and two B units struggle to handle a 21-car No. 77 through Carlsbad past the Buena Vista Wildlife Refuge on June 14, 1969. **Rick Peterson**

be considered in detail here. Amtrak's feeble beginnings were anything but smooth. Leased equipment, leased stations, cast-off people . . . but from this start, considerable progress was made in the intervening years.

When Amtrak took over the operation of the *San Diegans* in 1971, it operated two daily trains, and a tri-weekly connection to the then-new *Coast Starlight* (which runs Los Angeles to Seattle, combining three former trains). A novel feature of the new intercoastal service was through cars which operated all the way from San Diego to Seattle. They did not, however, operate in the same train all the way through; they were switched at Los Angeles. The number of through cars was limited by the size of the release track at Los Angeles, which could hold three cars and a switch engine. Most commonly this meant that two coaches and a sleeping car were the through cars. With a number of problems involved, including the time required to switch and turn the cars around at Los Angeles, the through service was quietly discontinued in January 1972. Since then, however, as there had been for years and years before, there is across-the-platform service, including transfer of checked baggage at Los Angeles. One could say it is almost the West Coast equivalent of "no passenger being able to pass through Chicago without changing trains."

F7A No. 342 models a rare version of the "pointless arrow" Amtrak emblem on start-up day, May 1, 1971. **John Shaw**

Above and at right: Early Amtrak trains appeared much as Santa Fe trains had for years. Amtrak No. 76 at Santa Ana on October 31, 1971, still looks like a Santa Fe operation, even down to the crew members' uniforms. Above right: Santa Fe S4 No. 1513 and caboose are tied up at the Santa Ana depot on that same day.
Three photos, Harry Spilman/ Dick Stephenson Collection

*Through cars from San Diego to the **Coast Starlight** on July 4, 1971, included Northern Pacific sleeping car No. 364 and a Southern Pacific 12-bedroom car. The through-car service was discontinued in January 1972.*
Dick Stephenson

Off to a Slow Start

Train frequency (three trains per day) stayed much the same from June 1972 until May 1976 when a State of California-supported train was added following the introduction of Amfleet equipment. Continued growth and expansion of the State support are covered in the next chapter.

A variety of equipment was used, in part because Amtrak experimented with some of the options available. In late 1972 ex-Santa Fe Hi-Level coaches were introduced, operating with low-level snack-lounge cars (ex-Santa Fe or CB&Q). Some ex-Southern Pacific coaches were used, before becoming the backbone of the fleet in 1974–75. They were often mixed with ex-Santa Fe cars, and augmented on occasion by stray ex-UP or even Seaboard Coast Line cars. The trains continued to look much the same as they had for many years.

At left: ***San Diegan*** *No. 770 heads south through Santa Ana on June 24, 1973, behind F7 Nos. 300C/300B/301A as the Fs near the end of their service on the* ***San Diegans;*** *soon they were displaced by brand-new SDP40Fs. The consist includes a mixture of ex-AT&SF, SP and CB&Q equipment. Below: Old meets new as two* ***San Diegans*** *meet at Miramar in July of 1973, and the engineer of the northbound (the F7) kids about hitching a ride.*
Clifford Prather; C.D. Finney/ Dick Stephenson Collection

Locomotive Changes

Motive power changed, too. The most significant development was the delivery of Amtrak's first new power, the SDP40Fs, in June 1973. These replaced leased Santa Fe F7s, which had served faithfully for many years. The familiar red and silver warbonnet was doomed by then, as the locomotives were either repainted in the interim blue and silver or yellow and silver schemes, or were rebuilt directly to CF7 roadswitchers at Santa Fe's Cleburne (Texas) Shops. No matter, as the "red nose" era had passed.

The SDPs were powerful, sleek and reliable. They were for a time assisted by ex-Burlington Northern F7Bs 398-399, and later by ex-Milwaukee Road E9Bs 451-452. An interesting change occurred in 1975 with the use of E9As 416-417. These were used singly, together, and with the B units, after the SDPs fell into disfavor due to a number of derailments. It was a case of David replacing Goliath. Already the handwriting was on the wall; Amfleet was on order, and the old equipment was to be moved aside to make way. Steam heating was on the way out, and the headend power concept was coming into full sway.

Performance Perceptions

Up until the gasoline crisis of 1974, many perceived the *San Diegans* to be merely a related service to other long-haul trains. They were a means of getting to and from a through train, and the schedules were built in a way to accommodate that purpose (south in the morning, north in the afternoon). It was not until a number of new riders were attracted to the route, and some other possibilities were explored, that the way in which the service was looked at was changed. Never mind that advertising was almost nil, or that the type in the timetable was so small that a magnifying glass was needed. While the *Coast Starlight, Southwest Limited* and *Sunset Limited* all built a passenger base, the *San Diegans* suffered, but (possibly) only because they had not yet been "discovered."

As can be seen in the next chapter, in the period from 1976 to the present the *San Diegans* have become a real success story in rail passenger travel.

Right: Ample power is available for train No. 772 as it sits at the San Diego depot on August 19, 1973. The 10 cars include privately owned ex-SP blunt-end sleeper No. 9027. Below: E9 Nos. 416/451 pause at Fullerton for the station stop in 1975. The Es worked into early 1976, when F40s and Amfleet cars arrived on the scene to take over.
Dick Stephenson;
Dick Stephenson Collection

3

To the Eighties and Beyond

IF ANYTHING CHARACTERIZES the current period of *San Diegan* service, it is the dramatic growth of ridership on the line. This has been brought about by the joint efforts of Amtrak and Caltrans, with a lot of "care and feeding."

This success story traces its roots back over a dozen years to when Caltrans began veering away from the policy of building bigger and better highways as the primary solution to intercity transportation needs. It is no coincidence that the predecessor name for this department was Division of Highways. The new name reflects a broadening of its mission.

In 1976, the Arab oil embargo was fresh in everyone's minds and was a decisive reason to look for alternative means of moving people between places. In this context (which was modified and reshaped in subsequent years) we approach the start of State of California support for *San Diegan* service. Technically, under Section 403b of the Rail Transportation Act, the states are empowered to share in the funding of intrastate service by paying a portion of the cost of operating a train. Three states have emerged over the years as leaders in these efforts: California, New York and Illinois. California has centered its efforts on two routes which, when taken together, form a spine or backbone of rail passenger service within the state from San Diego in the south, through to Stockton and Oakland in the north. Bus connections offer over 20 additional destinations from the *San Joaquins* and *San Diegans.* Few would have guessed in 1976 that the State-supported service would grow to become so popular and well-used.

An afternoon **San Diegan** *(No. 77) scoots along near Cardiff on November 28, 1976. Trains over seven cars long rate two F40s.* **John Shaw**

Growth for *San Diegans*

After the new Amfleet equipment was introduced in May of 1976, Caltrans and Amtrak collaborated on the joint funding of a fourth train on the line, established on Wednesday, September 1, 1976. This gave an additional round trip (trains 774 and 777) leaving Los Angeles at 4:10 P.M., returning from San Diego at 8:20 P.M.

With the new equipment it was easier to maintain the two-hour 35-minute schedule, and passengers could be assured that the air conditioning worked. While many railfans joked about the appearance of the new cars, they could not argue with their functionality. As crews got used to the new trainsets it was found that they could accelerate and brake rapidly, giving a degree of responsiveness not seen since the RDCs (which were as quick as jackrabbits). Ridership grew modestly between 1976 and 1977, and in April 1977, a fifth daily round trip was added, Nos. 778-779, with schedules shifted to add a midafternoon departure from Los Angeles, and a midmorning departure from San Diego. Again ridership grew (almost predictably) with the provision of additional options for travel.

The **El Camino** *heads south behind SDP40F 504 near Cardiff. Three coaches, a snack-lounge and a dome observation round out the consist, which served on the Surf Line for six months in 1978.* **John Shaw**

When Is a Commuter Not a Commuter?

Considerable space could be devoted to the issue of the Los Angeles County-owned train, sponsored by then-Supervisor Baxter Ward, which saw service on the Surf Line for a six-month period in 1978. In brief, the equipment was acquired from the Oregon, Pacific & Eastern Railway at Cottage Grove, Oregon. It had been used to carry tourists on a leisurely summer schedule on that shortline road; previous owners of the cars were Illinois Central, Milwaukee Road and Western Pacific. The 1973 gas crunch had made the issue of alternative modes of travel a hot topic. Baxter Ward, long a rail supporter, challenged the system, and withstood jibes of "Ward's Folly" and "Baxter's Choo-Choo." Long discussions with Amtrak and the Santa Fe Railway resulted in arbitration to determine what responsibilities Amtrak and Santa Fe had for operating commuter versus intercity service. In the end, a new train was added effective February 14, 1978, and was named the *El Camino*. The refurbished equipment, which was steam heated, became the trainset, pulled by SDP40F locomotives. This meant that other *San Diegan* equipment could not be operated on this train, and vice versa. At the end of the agreed-upon six-month period, the *El Camino* cars quietly went into storage (where they sat until sold to Mexico in 1987), and Caltrans stepped in to support the sixth daily *San Diegan* effective September 1978. Train numbers 770-780 and 771-781 were assigned.

The normal distinguishing features of commuter trains still do not seem to apply to *San Diegans,* such as frequent operations, many closely spaced stops and multi-ride tickets. Little can be found in advertisements which would even hint that these factors apply to *San Diegan* service.

More Growth

While frequency stayed the same from 1978 through October 26, 1980, ridership continued to climb as more and more passengers found the fast, frequent service to their liking. A seventh daily train was added on October 26, 1980, and for a growing number of people traveling on business, the train offered useful, timely service, more convenient than flying or driving.

In terms of farebox recovery (more correctly the revenue-to-cost ratio) the percentage steadily rose from 1976 onward, with a dip in the recession years of 1982–83. In 1988 it stood at 93 percent, and could conceivably go even higher. The State feels that its investment in the service has been money well spent. Even the money spent on advertising has brought additional ridership, and in numbers disproportionate to the dollar amounts spent.

Right: Heading west out of the Sorrento Valley, F40 No. 221 leads a ***San Diegan*** *under old Hwy. 101 at the Torrey Pines State Reserve south of Del Mar on August 8, 1978. Below: A northbound freight led by U36C No. 8775 skirts the edge of Doheny State Beach north of San Clemente on March 24, 1978. Freight business has played a decreasing role along the line in the past 10 years.*

Both photos, John Shaw

A rare event was a gas-crunch-inspired second section of a **San Diegan,** *seen southbound at Valencia in May of 1979. The two SDP40Fs had little trouble handling the five-car train, which included an ex-Burlington dome coach on the rear.*
Jim Minor

The 1984 experiment with Metroliner service was short-lived, but provided some helpful data. The concept was an extra-fare, limited-stop service on an expedited two-and-a-half-hour schedule, patterned after similar service in the Northeast Corridor. A complimentary newspaper and beverages were included. These perks carried through to the new Custom Class reserved first-class service introduced after the Metroliner was quietly phased out in the spring of 1985. Here was a way to attract business and professional people, on a route that travels through one of the highest per-capita income areas in the country: Orange County. Eureka! Custom Class was a hit, and today is well-used on a variety of schedules for many purposes.

Amtrak Takes Over Crews

One of the most significant changes in the operation of the *San Diegans* came in November 1986, when Amtrak took over train and engine crews. Substantial cost savings were realized by the move which made them direct employees of Amtrak. Major work rule changes meant that less money had to be spent on salaries, as the number of hours worked by each employee generally increased (since they are now paid on the basis of hours worked rather than miles operated). With the change, about half of the *San Diegan* runs are based in San Diego.

In a scene very typical of **San Diegans,** *No. 576 makes its station stop at San Juan Capistrano on July 12, 1987. Weekend trains frequently have two units and eight to twelve cars.*
Dick Stephenson

Traffic in both directions has come to a stop on busy I-5 in Irvine on August 27, 1988. The trains may be crowded, but the highways are more so. It is difficult to predict travel times. **Dick Stephenson**

Time Comparisons Passenger Car Versus Train

While preparing material for this book, I had the opportunity to compare travel time by car with the actual running time of a *San Diegan* on more than one occasion. One time was July 16, 1988, an average Saturday, with the usual midday congestion on Interstate 5, just before the Del Mar racing season.

I left Los Angeles at the same time as No. 774 (10:45 A.M.). Since I was equipped with a scanner radio, I was able to monitor its progress along the route. Number 774 had F40s 224 and 214 and ten cars. On the way south, No. 774 met No. 577 at Orange, and No. 579 at Fallbrook Junction, just north of Oceanside.

On Interstate 5, there was stop-and-go traffic between Anaheim and San Juan Capistrano. Speeds on the highway varied between zero and 65. On arrival in San Diego, I had a ten-minute lead over the train, but it had been quite a trip. If motorists don't absolutely have to have their cars once they arrive in San Diego, leaving the driving to someone else seems like a better idea, considering traffic and stressful conditions.

A slightly different comparison was made while following No. 581 northward on that same day, from Del Mar to Fullerton, overtaking it at Oceanside, seeing it again at San Clemente and at Orange. While the train may reach higher speeds than highway vehicles, the station stops and other operating restrictions take their toll in time, reducing average speed. A two-hour thirty-minute schedule by rail requires nearly a fifty-mile-per-hour average speed . . . something difficult to attain.

	No. 774		
	(Schedule)	(Actual)	Highway
Los Angeles	10:45 a.m.	10:45 a.m.	
Commerce		11:05	11:05**
Fullerton	11:17		—
Anaheim Stadium	11:27	11:39	11:39
Santa Ana	11:38	11:59	11:55
Irvine			12:03 p.m.
San Juan Capistrano	12:01 p.m.	12:25 p.m.	12:42
San Clemente	12:15		12:52
Oceanside	12:40	1:06	1:09
Del Mar	12:56	1:23	—
Mission Bay		1:47	1:37
San Diego	1:40	1:56	1:45

****I-5 crossing at Garfield Avenue.**

Number 583 gets ready for departure from San Diego on May 7, 1988. Trains operating in the push mode northbound never have been the norm, although occasionally they are seen. The push-pull concept is designed to save time in turning trainsets at San Diego. **Dick Stephenson**

The Eighth Train Threshold

For some time it was a goal of various groups and agencies to see an eighth daily train added. After some discussions about equipment, schedules, and the availability of sidings for trains to meet, an agreement was reached so that effective October 29, 1987, the eighth train could begin operation. After appropriate ceremonies at San Diego on October 29, the eight-daily train schedule commenced.

Push-Pull Trains

The introduction of push-pull equipment, using cab cars to control the operation of the train in the "push" (locomotive trailing) mode made shortened turnaround times possible. The cab cars were rebuilt at Amtrak's Wilmington, Delaware, Shops from the original Metroliners, later known as Capitoliners, which had their electrical equipment removed and became coaches with a control compartment.

Cab car No. 9633 leads train No. 572 out of LAUPT in June 1988, before the cab cars were removed from leading consists due to brake valve problems.
Dick Stephenson

Train No. 571 (dubbed "the commuter") has just about completed its journey as it passes Macy St. in Los Angeles on a July morning in 1988. Construction in the background is for the extension of the El Monte Busway, which also affects depot trackage at Los Angeles. **Dick Stephenson**

They were not an immediate hit with passengers or crews, some of which even referred to them as "coffin" cars (a term which was not hung on them because of a fatal accident, but due to an alliteration of the Custom Class car that passengers have become accustomed to finding on one end of the train). Since as of mid-1988 their enhanced collision protection had not been tested in a major grade-crossing accident, many crewmen were skeptical about the way in which these cars might react. A brake valve problem in July 1988 did little to reassure those involved with the *San Diegan* service that these were reliable cars.

Another change that took place when push-pull was instituted was that half the seats in each car were permanently faced in each direction, so that they need not be turned. Much like commuter equipment, some of the passengers are at any given time riding backwards.

Onward to Santa Barbara

The concept of a San Diego-to-Santa Barbara corridor had long been considered by Caltrans . . . over a dozen years at this writing. Certainly in looking at where the population is distributed, it is not just south and east of Los Angeles. With two operating railroads to deal with, the proposals for through service were viewed by at least two sets of jaundiced eyes. Coordination of the service was not at all easy. It was through marked determination, and only after overcoming a number of obstacles (many of which were political), that the service was finally established on June 26, 1988, as trains 774 and 783. These used existing schedules from the *San Diegan* group and added a 700-series prefix to identify them as through trains. The fact that Amtrak crews operated the trains, even with a crew change in Los Angeles, served to make the transition between the two railroads easier. If anything, the sometimes stodgy Southern Pacific, not well known for its cooperation in passsenger operation projects, has been very helpful in the operation of the new Santa Barbara service. Many of the late train operations that have been experienced have been due to the San Diego end of the run, not the Southern Pacific portion. Ridership on the new run was very encouraging in the early weeks. National Association of Railroad Passenger sources indicated that the Santa Barbara portion of the service handled 11,000 passengers during the month of July 1988, more than some entire routes did. Caltrans has asked Amtrak to add a second

Selected Annual San Diegan *Ridership*

Year	Ridership	Year	Ridership
1947	1,026,389	1979	1,123,000
1952	1,260,000	1980	1,233,000
1962	547,000	1981	1,202,000
1971	335,000	1982	1,190,000
1973	328,000	1983	1,159,000
1974	390,000	1984	1,222,000
1975	355,000	1985	1,290,000
1976	405,000	1986	1,415,000
1977	690,000	1987	1,491,000
1978	794,000	1988 (est.)	1,675,000

Sources: Amtrak, Caltrans, Santa Fe Railway.

Train No. 774 inbound from Santa Barbara pauses at Glendale on July 17, 1988, behind F40s 221/229. Due to brake valve problems there is no cab car in the consist, and the two units ran around the train in Santa Barbara. Patronage on the Santa Barbara side was good in the first few months of service. **Dick Stephenson**

Train Numbers for San Diegans

Train numbers on the Surf Line have always been in the 70 series. Looking as far back as 1896, California Southern Railway numbered their trains in this series.

During the last fifty years, Santa Fe also numbered the *San Diegans* in the 70s. When Amtrak first took over the service in 1971, numbers did not change. After November 11, 1971, a national numbering series was adopted, and the *San Diegans* retained their heritage, using the 70 series as a suffix. Train numbers from then to October 26, 1980, were in the 770s. After that they became the 570s and 580s. Numbers as high as 590-591 have been assigned (for the seasonal Del Mar service in 1987).

In 1988 the two trains operating between San Diego and Santa Barbara were assigned numbers 774 and 783 to differentiate them from the other trains which operate only between San Diego and Los Angeles.

In its operating timetable Santa Fe has always referred to the trains by their two-digit numbers. So, no matter what the prefix, they are still consistently identified by the railroad. It's a heritage that's been around a long time, and is still going strong.

Santa Barbara round trip. It will be interesting to see if the patronage meets expectations, and if the projected third daily round trip being talked about by planners can be justified.

The Santa Barbara extension added six stops new to *San Diegan* service: Glendale*, Van Nuys, Chatsworth, Simi Valley*, Oxnard* and Santa Barbara*. A seventh is being developed at Ventura. The four marked with asterisks are shared with the *Coast Starlight*. There have been a number of discussions regarding the Burbank Airport stop adjacent to Hollywood-Burbank Airport and Lockheed Aircraft, with no agreement reached by mid-1988 for use of the stop. This station, like those at Van Nuys and Chatsworth, was put in by Caltrans as part of the 1982 Oxnard Commuter Project, so the platforms were there and ready when Santa Barbara *San Diegan* service started.

LOSSAN Signifies Progress

When improvements to the San Diego line were being considered in 1987, a joint study committee found an innovative way to fund the project. Caltrans, Amtrak and Santa Fe had long been working cooperatively together to bring about a combination of equipment, service and station improvements. Building on that cooperation, the Counties of Los Angeles, Orange and San Diego were added to the mix, sharing in the consideration of rail service as a transportation alternative, and providing sales/gas tax revenues to be used for improvements. What grew out of the joint agency agreement was the funding for Phase I of the San Diego improvement project, covering new rail and roadway work for the 12 miles between Fullerton and East Santa Ana.

This was significant because this was the first time that

Left: There is considerable evidence of the rail project in this shot of No. 580 passing the Orange depot on July 16, 1988. The project management trailer can be seen at right. Below: The work train is tied up at Orange on July 23, 1988. Trackwork was done at night to reduce delays.

Both photos, Dick Stephenson

local entities, rather than just the State, were sharing in the cost of upgrading rail facilities. The Santa Fe Railway probably would not have been able to justify the cost of the new welded rail which has been laid had it not been for the assistance with the funding. Participation is Caltrans 50 percent, and Amtrak, Santa Fe and each of the three Counties 10 percent. This same formula will be carried through in subsequent phases of the project. Phase II from East Santa Ana to Serra (near San Juan Capistrano) is tentatively slated to begin in spring 1989.

Projections for *San Diegans* into the Nineties

Assuming that facility improvements (including additional sidings) are funded and additional equipment is made available, it is safe to project that there will be ten daily *San Diegans* in the early 1990s. For ease in remembering the schedule, hourly departures for the better part of the day may well be the mark of the service. This has been a successful ploy for the intrastate airlines that seemingly compete with the Amtrak service. As highway congestion grows closer to the completely clogged level, alternatives such as the *San Diegan* take on more importance. The rail service runs 365 days a year, rain or shine, and serves a broad segment of the traveling public. Whether for business or pleasure travel, the *San Diegans* will be there and ready.

Population

1986 Population Estimates for on-line *San Diegan* cities:

City	Population
Los Angeles	3,790,000
Fullerton	112,000
Anaheim	243,000
Orange	102,000
Santa Ana	232,000
Irvine	88,000
El Toro	42,000
San Juan Capistrano	19,000
San Clemente	32,000
Oceanside	148,000
Carlsbad	46,000
Encinitas	42,000
Del Mar	5,000
San Diego	1,035,000

Source: Rand McNally Commercial Atlas, 1988 edition.

***San Diegan** No. 578 pauses on August 19, 1988, to mark the centennial of the completion of the Surf Line near El Toro. Amtrak Western Director of Public Affairs Arthur Lloyd; Darrell Brewer, Chairman of the Southern California Chapter of the Railway and Locomotive Historical Society; Don Hofsommer of the Lexington Group; John Berry, President of the Santa Fe Railway Historical Society; and Mike Martin, Special Representative of the Public Relations Department of Santa Fe Railway represented their organizations in observing the event. Santa Fe Track Inspection Car 89 was on the rear of the train for Lexingtonians and invited guests. Left and below: One benefit of the LOSSAN track improvement project was the extension of Anaheim siding. Seen here from Santa Fe Track Inspection Car 89 on August 19, 1988, the new west switch and skeleton track can be seen prior to completion of the siding extension.* **Three photos, Dick Stephenson**

Notable Dates in San Diegan *Service*

August 12, 1888	**Line completed between Oceanside and Fullerton, golden spike driven near what is now El Toro.**
January 1915	**New San Diego depot opens.**
March 27, 1938	***San Diegan* service begun with new lightweight trainset, two round trips per day.**
May 7, 1939	**Los Angeles Union Passenger Terminal opens.**
June 8, 1941	**Second lightweight *San Diegan* set enters service.**
December 7, 1946	**New Oceanside depot opened.**
April 1, 1947	**Through sleeper service started between Washington, D.C., and San Diego (via *Chief* and B&O).**
1949	**GM *Train of Tomorrow* on display.**
May 21, 1952	**RDC cars enter service, two round trips per day.**
August 23, 1953	**Last steam run by engine 3751 (4-8-4) on trains 72-73.**
June 6, 1954	**Through sleeper discontinued.**
January 22, 1956	**Tragic RDC wreck at Redondo Junction, Los Angeles, 30 killed, 174 injured.**
March 1956	**GM Aerotrain on display, makes eight trips.**
July 4, 1956	**New *El Capitan* equipment displayed at San Diego.**
October 28, 1957	**Service reduced to five daily trains plus one additional round trip on weekends.**
November 19, 1958	**Marine jet (F4D Skyray) hits No. 74 near Irvine.**
July 1, 1964	**Mail contract not renewed.**
Labor Day 1965	**Two 23-car Del Mar Race trains operated.**
September 29, 1965	**Service reduced to three trains each way, final level under Santa Fe.**
December 22, 1965	**Truck collides with No. 76 in Anaheim, units 51C/61 badly damaged, retired; one killed, 40 injured.**
July, August 1966	**Airline strike, extra sections operated, last major use of heavyweights.**
May 1, 1971	**Amtrak takes over operation of service, two trains daily plus tri-weekly connection to *Coast Starlight,* initiates through-car service to Seattle.**
January 12, 1972	**Through-car service dropped.**
June 19, 1972	**Service returned to three daily trains.**
January 1976	***Freedom Train* displayed at Miramar and San Juan Capistrano.**
May 25, 1976	**Amfleet equipment introduced.**
September 1, 1976	**Fourth daily round trip added (403b).**
April 24, 1977	**Fifth daily round trip added (403b).**
February 14, 1978	**Sixth daily round trip added (Los Angeles County).**
September 1978	**Sixth daily round trip (continued 403b).**
October 26, 1980	**Seventh daily round trip added (Amtrak), train numbers changed from 770s to 570s.**
March 13-14, 1982	**Amtrak Family Days—San Diego.**
May 1984	**New Anaheim Stadium Station dedicated.**
August 1985	**Connecting bus service started.**
September 7, 1985	**New Santa Ana Transportation Center opened.**
April 26-27, 1986	**Travel and Vacation Show—San Diego.**
October 29, 1987	**Eighth daily train added (403b), push-pull officially starts.**
January 31, 1988	**Super Bowl XXII in San Diego.**
May 5-7, 1988	**San Diego RailFair.**
June 26, 1988	**One trip per day extended to Santa Barbara.**
August 19, 1988	**Centennial of completion of line observed.**

Amtrak

4

Special Movements

WHILE THE FOCUS OF THIS BOOK is on *San Diegan* service, a number of other movements and specials have taken place along the Surf Line. We obviously do not have the space to detail each and every one, but some significant ones have found their way into both the text and photos. They add spice.

Del Mar Race Trains

Del Mar Racetrack opened in 1937, so its existence nearly parallels that of the *San Diegans*. Located 105 rail miles south of Los Angeles, the racetrack has been a popular rail destination over the years. It was an easy walk from trainside to the grandstand. The special trains were turned and spotted at an adjacent wye, returning to Los Angeles late in the afternoon.

For many years the race trains used heavyweight equipment. When these were in short supply, even Tourist sleepers were used in coach service. Motive power ran the gambit, from steam to Geeps to cab units.

The last Del Mar Race Special operated Labor Day 1969, ending the long era of that service by Santa Fe.

The first of seven turbo sets ordered by Amtrak from Rohr Industries (Chula Vista, California) heads north along the Surf Line on May 29, 1976. The remains of the siding at the old San Clemente station can be seen in the foreground; in the background is the San Clemente Pier, location of the present stop. This set stopped off at the D.O.T. test track in Pueblo, Colorado, before continuing on to its new home in Rensselaer, New York. **Steve Patterson**

Branchline Specials

During the sixties fantrips on the two branch lines off the Surf Line were popular. They made excellent one-day excursions from either Los Angeles or San Diego. A number were operated to Fallbrook; others reached Escondido and the Venta Spur.

During the seventies the operating costs for one-day trips skyrocketed, becoming prohibitive. Pacific Railroad Society sponsored one excursion on the Surf Line from Los Angeles to Oceanside and return on May 21, 1977, using Hi-Level equipment.

Santa Fe operated its own special trains from time to time, specifically to San Diego for the Board of Directors in May 1985, and to Del Mar for invited guests in August 1985, 1986 and 1987. It also operated a special train to San Diego for the Super Bowl game on January 31, 1988.

Private Cars Also Popular

The movement of private cars on the rear of *San Diegans* is not something that was started by Amtrak. The pricing of such moves has changed, however, as the railroad charged 18 first-class fares per car, while Amtrak imposed a per-mile charge. The popularity of such moves picked up in the mid-sixties when cars such as 1509, *Golden West, Cyrus K. Holliday* and *Victoria* were regulars.

In the early seventies, cars such as *Cyrus K. Holliday, Afton Canyon,* 6101 and 5001 were often seen. The market grew in the eighties. Cars that have frequented the line recently include *Native Son, Silver Patio, La Condesa,* 5011, *Cyrus K. Holliday* and occasionally the 1509 or *Robert Peary.*

For many travelers, the private car provides a way to experience the luxury of an earlier time in rail travel. It shows how comfort and the camaraderie of a group can enhance a trip.

Left: Steam power from two eras combine on a troop train in 1948, as 2-10-2 No. 1625 couples on to help 4-8-4 No. 2903 up the 2.2 percent grade to Linda Vista. Below: General Motors' ***Train of Tomorrow*** *visited San Diego in 1949 as part of a nation-wide tour. E7 765 carried cab signals, and also was fitted with an ATS shoe for her trip along the Surf Line. As popular as dome cars became, they never were regularly assigned on the Surf route.* **Both photos, R.P. Middlebrook/ Stan Kistler Collection**

Above: GP7 2651 shows its muscle as it crests the grade at Linda Vista (Miramar) in 1952 with a 10-car train of tourist Pullmans. (Amtrak F40s are rated for seven cars on the same grade today.) Right: Another General Motors experiment was the ***Aerotrain,*** *which AT&SF hosted in 1956. Here the demo set heads through Orange, as the engineer intently watches the camera.* **R.P. Middlebrook/ Stan Kistler Collection; Ed Workman/John Signor Collection**

*Above: A Del Mar racetrack special, running along the beach at San Clemente at 70 mph, had 10 heavyweight coaches in tow on June 16, 1946. Below: The public always enjoys a display, and this 1950 Santa Fe event in San Diego was no exception. Beside the regular **San Diegan** (with one of the chair-observations carrying the drumhead) are 0-4-0 **Little Buttercup** and F3 set No. 18, while in the left background is a Santa Fe business car.*

John L. Whitmeyer/Bob Kern Collection; Santa Fe Railway

The Del Mar racetrack opened in 1937, so its life nearly parallels that of **San Diegan** *service. The proximity of rails to the grandstands enhanced Santa Fe's role in the annual summer racing meeting at the place "Where the surf meets the turf." Here, dual-service F7 set 326 heads around the wye with one of the 90-class RPO-coach cars on July 24, 1953. Note the green flags, which denote the special had operated as a section of a regular train (probably No. 74).*
John Shaw

Recent changes in Amtrak operating procedures have made the use of privately owned cars more difficult. Within two years, private cars will have to be equipped with headend power and multiple-unit cables, so that they can be placed anywhere in the consist. This represents an additional expense for car owners. Notwithstanding that, we expect to see private cars operated to San Diego for some time to come.

Above: When coaches ran short, tourist Pullmans were used in coach service, as shown here on September 7, 1953, at Del Mar where GP7 No. 2650 awaits its return trip to Los Angeles. Left: Not as rare a shot as it might seem, No. 257L and a booster lead a race train on September 5, 1953, at Del Mar. The B unit is equipped with a steam boiler, and the A unit with steam lines.
Both photos, John Shaw

Above: In a scene that cannot be repeated today, a four-unit set of Fs led by No. 340 handles a late sixties excursion at Fallbrook. Right: Not two sections of the same train, No. 75 pauses at Oceanside in July 1970 alongside the Trainmen's Picnic Special (right) which carried employees and their families to the beach at Oceanside for the day. By this time the F7s were looking a bit worn . . . Amtrak was nine months away.

Both photos, Rick Peterson

Above: The United Aircraft turbo pauses at Del Mar on July 24, 1971, as a part of its demonstration tour. Amtrak eventually bought turbotrains, but not for the Surf Line. Right: Ex-SP blunt end sleeper No. 9027 made its maiden run under private ownership to San Diego on August 19, 1973. The classic Budd-built car continues on in service, but will never be quite the same as when it carried the markers on the ***Sunset Limited*** *or the* ***Cascade.*** *Below: A privately owned car seen frequently on* ***San Diegans*** *in the sixties and seventies was ex-AT&SF cafe-lounge-observation 1509. The car is now owned by the San Diego Railway Historical Society and based at Campo, California. It was photographed here on April 12, 1980, at San Diego before returning to Los Angeles.*

Rick Peterson; Dick Stephenson; John Shaw

Right: The coach yard foreman hasn't lost his marbles. This special train made three round trips to San Diego on January 20, 21, 22, 1977, to film TV commercials both inside and outside the train. SDP40F 504 leads the unique train which includes a Hi-level coach, ex-SP coach, baggage car and ex-AT&SF diner and coaches at San Juan Capistrano on January 20, 1977. Below: Pacific Railroad Society's excursion train to Oceanside rests in that city while passengers are bused through nearby Camp Pendleton on May 21, 1977.

Steve Patterson;
Dick Stephenson

Above: Santa Fe-Southern Pacific Corporation's Security Analysts' Special lays over at San Diego on April 25, 1984. FP45 No. 5996 had help from two other speedsters of the same ex-passenger class as the train covered the Surf Line, Cajon Pass and Tehachapi all in the same day. Below right: Ready to break the banner at the opening of the Santa Ana Regional Transportation Center is F40 No. 214 on September 7, 1985. The new depot has been referred to alternately as a showplace or a cathedral. It is an impressive structure which provides access to a number of modes of travel. Below left: Amtrak's display during the Vacation and Travel Show in San Diego on April 25-26, 1986, included Amfleet, Superliners and an exhibit car (converted baggage car 10090).

David Busse; Rich Thurman/RailPAC; Dick Stephenson

Above: Ex-UP dorm-lounge No. 6102 lays over in San Diego on February 4, 1973. Note the train of high-level equipment behind the baggage car, serving as the ***San Diegan*** *that day. Right: Ex-Soo Line No. 52, renamed* ***Cyrus K. Holliday,*** *was long a fixture at the coach yard across from the San Diego depot. It is shown here on February 4, 1973. Below: This is* ***not*** *push-pull with the* ***Native Son*** *as a buffer! A car was added to No. 583, then the private car was spotted on the next track over for No. 585. The date: July 23, 1988, at San Diego.*

Three photos, Dick Stephenson

Above: One of many privately owned cars to ply the Surf Line in recent years, converted sleeping car ***Yerba Buena*** *graces the end of* ***San Diegan*** *No. 576 on August 27, 1988, at Fullerton. Right: The* ***Cyrus K. Holliday*** *rounds the bend at Mission Tower on June 22, 1988, bringing up the rear of No. 578.*

Both photos, Dick Stephenson

5

Along the Line Today

IN THE FIFTY YEARS OF *San Diegan* service a number of things have changed. While the trains are still plying the route between the two major Southern California cities of Los Angeles and San Diego, there certainly are many more people who have access to the line, and the entire transportation scene has drastically shifted from the days when trains were the primary means of travel for many people. This was particularly true in the teens and twenties, before the good roads we today take so much for granted were built.

In 1938 trains originated and terminated at Santa Fe's fine La Grande Station at Second Street and Santa Fe Avenue, on the east side of the downtown area of Los Angeles. Streetcar service brought travelers right to the front door. Until May 7, 1939, this was Santa Fe's address in Los Angeles, after which passenger operations for all three railroads in town shifted to the long-awaited, and often-fought-over Los Angeles Union Passenger Terminal. This magnificent depot today retains much of the splendor it had when it opened nearly fifty years ago. Many rail historians feel that we are lucky to have such a notable station complex still available and active today.

*The Surf Line fits neatly into the coastal scene, exemplified here by trackage along the bluffs in Del Mar at MP 246 on July 16, 1988. At this location (near where the cover shot for this book was taken), joggers, surfers and **San Diegans** freely interface.* **Dick Stephenson**

The depot in San Diego can just as readily be pointed to as a noteworthy landmark and edifice. From its opening in 1915 (see photo on page 12) until 1951, it could legitimately be called a union station, because trains of the San Diego & Arizona (later the San Diego & Arizona Eastern) operated from it as well as those of the Santa Fe. For many years now the *Santa Fe* sign atop the depot has left little doubt as to who is the major railroad in town. Hundreds of thousands of travelers have passed through this mission-style depot, particularly many servicemen headed to or from a variety of duty stations. Despite proposed plans to erect an office complex on its site, the historic structure survives today and continues to serve the large numbers of passengers who use it every day.

In 1938 when *San Diegan* service started, the new lightweight, fast trains made only three intermediate stops—Santa Ana, Oceanside and Del Mar. By 1950, Del Mar was downgraded to a flag stop. In 1955, five stops were scheduled: Rivera, Fullerton, Santa Ana, Oceanside and Del Mar. The two round trips operated by the Rail Diesel Cars (RDCs) met a two and one-half hour schedule and made nine stops: Fullerton, Anaheim and Orange (flag stops), Santa Ana, San Juan Capistrano (flag), San Clemente (flag), Oceanside, Encinitas (flag) and Del Mar. That running time yields a fifty-mph average including stops, something that would be difficult to sustain today.

By 1963 each of the five daily trains was stopping at different stations. The midmorning departure of No. 74, for example, made ten stops including flag stops, and had a running time of three hours. The Sunday/Holiday sched-

Above left: With push-pull **San Diegans** *it's hard to know whether they are coming or going. Number 580 heads under the Hollywood-Santa Ana Freeway (U.S. 101) on September 2, 1988, with an extra heavy load of Labor Day weekend travelers. The construction on the edge of the freeway is for the extension of the El Monte Busway, which also altered the appearance of the platforms and trainsheds at Los Angeles Union Passenger Terminal. Above right: F40 No. 222 pushes No. 578 past Hobart Tower on August 27, 1988. The tower protects the crossing of UP's Harbor line with the AT&SF San Bernardino Subdivision, and is UP's last manned tower in California.* **Both photos, Dick Stephenson**

ule for Nos. 79 and 80 made five stops in the two-hour and forty-minute run.

By 1967, with service reduced to three trains each way each day, about half of the ten intermediate stops were conditional, and normal running time was two hours fifty-five minutes. There were times, however, that a train could arrive a few minutes early, if it had a good run.

Along the Line Today

Assuming that you will be making a southbound (railroad-eastbound) trip along the route of the *San Diegan* today, what will you be likely to see?

Starting with Los Angeles Union Passenger Terminal, you can enter through the impressive high-ceilinged waiting room, or you can buy your ticket in the adjacent wing at the ticket counters that are located today right where they have been for fifty years. The door to the tunnel still announces the train name that has been familiar to millions of passengers—*San Diegan.* When the door is opened for boarding, you will join the throng of passengers for the brisk walk down the tunnel and then up the ramp indicated for your train. After getting aboard the train and finding a seat, you will wait for departure time.

Over the years the practice has alternated between heading and backing out of Union Station. If your train backs out, it may be somewhat disorienting to you as you travel around the big curve outside the depot, and past Mission Tower (alongside the big DWP [Department of Water & Power] maintenance yard) before heading south along the Los Angeles River. No matter whether the train heads or backs out, the line then follows the river for three miles, passing the old Santa Fe First Street Yard (soon to be the MetroRail Maintenance Facility), Amtrak's Eighth Street Coach Yard, and Redondo Junction Roundhouse. This is where Amtrak equipment for long-haul trains as well as for *San Diegans* is maintained. After completing the big sweeping curve at Redondo Junction Tower and

Located on the east side of Alameda Street east of the Plaza and historic Olvera Street, Los Angeles Union Passenger Terminal is closer to Downtown and three freeways than some might expect. The main structure itself has changed little in its fifty years, though entrance ways and parking areas have continued to change since this July 1975 view. Metrorail (Los Angeles' downtown subway) will provide a station under the station when completed. **Dick Stephenson**

crossing the river, the line snakes between industries as it heads generally southeast, crossing Union Pacific's Harbor Branch at Hobart Tower (UP's last tower in California). Train speeds increase as Santa Fe's main freight yard, Hobart Yard, slips by on the left side. The main line crosses the Santa Ana Freeway (I-5) near Garfield Avenue, site of the proposed new Commerce station.

After years of effort, all grade crossings have been separated or eliminated between Los Angeles and Pico Rivera. Your train will speed along, slowing only for the crossings of Southern Pacific trackage at Los Nietos. The line then curves south through Santa Fe Springs (an area known over the years for its petroleum production) before

Above: The new Commerce station is to be built here adjacent to 26th St. and Garfield Ave. (a location known as Lever Bros. for the nearby soap manufacturer) where the new third main track currently ends. The tracks crest in this view at the bridge over I-5. Left: A classic suburban station, Rivera (later Pico Rivera) served for many years. As seen here in September 1962, the depot had another nine years of service before being moved away for non-railroad uses. Only the palm trees remain today to mark the location.

Dick Stephenson; John Shaw

This unique perspective provides a good idea of what DT Junction is all about. Besides crossing the San Gabriel River and the Southern Pacific Puente branch at grade, Slauson Ave. crosses over, grade separated, and beyond is a pair of crossovers and the underpass for the I-605 Freeway.
Dick Stephenson Collection

Fullerton station has changed little over the years, whether shown by this 1960 shot of a westbound ***San Diegan*** *behind F7 No. 340, or a current August 1988 shot of the station complex, with the UP's Fullerton depot (formerly located across the Santa Fe tracks) in the background. The UP depot is now an Old Spaghetti Factory restaurant.* **Santa Fe Railway; Dick Stephenson**

Above: Built new by Amtrak, Anaheim Stadium station sits in the parking lot of the stadium, as seen here on July 7, 1988. Above right: The right-of-way south of Orange is narrow, seen here on July 23, 1988. After crossing over Fairhaven Avenue, in the distance, the tracks of the Surf Line are about 20 feet from the backyards of houses, along Lincoln Ave.

Dick Stephenson; Dick Stephenson Collection

curving to the east again, going through La Mirada, passing Fullerton Airport, crossing the UP's Anaheim Branch at Basta, and heading into the heavily used Fullerton depot.

Fullerton to Santa Ana

Fullerton Station is a classic of Spanish design, reminiscent of the long-established Santa Fe Southwest heritage. The stucco and tile depot is owned now by the City of Fullerton, and is a true transportation center providing connections between several forms of transportation.

From Los Angeles to Fullerton the line is the San Bernardino Subdivision of Santa Fe's California Division. This is big-time railroading, with multiple tracks, reverse signaling, and high traffic density. Leaving Fullerton, the San Diego line branches off to the south, just east of the station. From this point the San Diego Subdivision covers the 102 miles to San Diego, mostly with single track. Currently there are ten intermediate sidings and six stations.

Through Anaheim the right-of-way is narrow, and fits right between the buildings. The Southern Pacific Tustin branch is crossed just north of Anaheim Stadium station. This station, which was opened in 1984, is located immediately adjacent to the stadium complex (home of the California Angels and Los Angeles Rams) and just west of the California Highway 57 freeway. The modern station building sits down below track level on the right side of the tracks, nestled among eucalyptus trees, with some very nice landscaping.

After pausing to pick up additional passengers, your train will ease across the Santa Ana River, and make a sweeping right-hand turn south through the center of Orange. The depot here is still standing, but is no longer used by passengers. After threading its way between houses, and along the very narrow right-of-way adjacent to Lincoln Avenue, your train will arrive at the impressive Santa Ana Transportation Center.

Old Santa Ana depot was appreciated by passengers and fans alike. Seen here on October 31, 1971, the station continued to serve until 1985. It was later razed.

Harry Spilman/Dick Stephenson Collection

Neo-classic Mission Beauty

For years Santa Fe's modest stucco depot on East Fourth Street in Santa Ana was well used, and popular with passengers and railfans alike. Here one could park and ride, or merely sit and watch, as the mood struck. The prospect of joint funding to construct a true transportation center appealed to local officials. The impressive depot that resulted is testimony to a vision. It set an example of what can be done when there is local cooperation. Served

The new Santa Ana Transportation Center stands as a monument to the rebirth of the Surf Line's popularity. **Jim Walker**

by long-haul and regional buses on the west side, Amtrak trains glide effortlessly to a halt on the depot's east side, providing compatibility between the modes. The depot also contains shops and a restaurant. The detailing of the building, with its mission styling, is impressive.

The Speedway

Leaving Santa Ana, the line curves gently to the southeast, and double track extends southward for four miles, allowing the train to accelerate to 90 mph, its authorized maximum speed. Back in the passenger portion of the train, you may not even notice how fast you are traveling unless you have a reference point.

Inveterate train riders know that those trackside posts with a number affixed are an important reference point. Not only do they give you a specific location, but by timing the distance between mileposts one can gauge the train's speed. At 60 mph, it's a mile a minute; at 75 mph a mile slips by in 48 seconds, and at 90, in 40 seconds. Imagine my surprise when, as a youngster of 10 riding the *San Diegan,* my grandfather proudly took out his pocket watch and showed me how to make this calculation! It was like being inducted into a secret order.

On the San Diego line, mileposts start at mile 140 at Mission Tower in Los Angeles, and run to mile 267 in San Diego.

New Irvine Station

Armed with this newfound information, you can now relate to the location of the new Irvine station (opening in late 1989) as being near milepost 185. (Some people will find it easier to understand that it will be off Barranca Road, adjacent to the El Toro Marine Air Station.) This location culminates many years of discussion as to where a stop should be located in this rapidly growing area.

The line continues south between and behind various light industrial and commercial buildings in El Toro before heading through a small canyon and crossing under Interstate 5 near La Paz Road. Up to the left is Mission Viejo, a group of developments of the late sixties and early seventies. Continuing south, the line passes what remains of Rancho Capistrano (one of the last areas that still has orange groves, reminding visitors of what much of Southern California was like before houses became the largest cash crop each year, and the freeway became king).

San Juan Capistrano

The train arrives at San Juan Capistrano depot right in the center of this historic community, within easy walking distance of the Mission. In 1975 the depot was converted to a restaurant with a railroad theme, which includes old railroad equipment (such as ex-Santa Fe baggage-library-lounge 1300, and a Santa Fe caboose). A large number of commuters from surrounding communities now board the trains at this point.

Leaving Capistrano, the train eases across San Juan Creek (a watercourse which is normally docile, but which from time to time becomes angry with runoff waters). Serra siding near the Coast Highway is frequently used as a meeting point for trains, as it stands almost exactly at the halfway point between San Diego and Los Angeles.

Past Serra the line crosses Highway 1, and parallels it for four miles along the bluffs before the highway turns inland to run through the center of San Clemente. The tracks are

Left: Passengers await the arrival of No. 581 at San Juan Capistrano on August 19, 1988. The depot has been a restaurant since 1975, with passing trains just an added bit of local color. Below: The old San Clemente depot (see page 90) was adjacent to El Camino Real (Pacific Coast Highway) until closed in 1960; the stop was subsequently moved 1.1 miles south to the pier. This July 1988 view shows the site, plus the heavy rip-rap Santa Fe has placed there to keep tracks and water separated.
Both photos, Dick Stephenson

right on the edge of the sand . . . for the next forty-five miles. This is what the Surf Line is best known for, even though it comprises only about one third of the total mileage between Los Angeles and San Diego.

San Clemente—Old and New

San Clemente is the southernmost city in Orange County. It is a well-to-do community which has always been home to many wealthy residents . . . even a President (Richard M. Nixon). While little of the town itself can be seen from the train, be assured that the property values are high here. Considerable growth in the last fifteen years has added many hillside homes.

In addition to the affluence mentioned above, San Clemente has a fine beach and pier. For years the swimming and surfing here have attracted many people, especially youngsters, from all over the region. Santa Fe and Amtrak have handled significant numbers who chose to ride to and from this beach aboard the train.

Before 1960, passengers debarked and boarded trains at a fine stucco depot a mile and a quarter north of the San Clemente Pier. Today trains stop at the pier, and though there is no fancy structure, and only two trains each way each day stop here, the location works well.

In the stretch along the beachfront, train speed is limited to 40 mph, and for good reason, as there are many people who cross the right-of-way to get to and from the beach. South of San Clemente, the line crosses San Mateo and San Onofre Creeks. Both of these locations have been washed out from time to time due to the runoff which pours down from the hills in torrents.

On the right at San Onofre is the Southern California Edison nuclear generating plant with its twin-domed reactors.

A few miles south on the left (on Interstate 5) is the Border Patrol inspection point where northbound vehicular traffic is checked.

Camp Pendleton

One of the few open areas along the line is the fifteen miles between San Onofre and Oceanside. This military reservation is the site of the U.S. Marine Corps advanced infantry training, home of the First Marine Division, and site of Marine, and joint Naval and Marine exercises.

Along this stretch the speed limit of 90 allows trains to demonstrate their superiority over vehicular traffic on paralleling Interstate 5.

LOS ANGELES
REDONDO JCT.
HOBART
RIVERA
SANTA FE SPRINGS
LA MIRADA
FULLERTON
ATWOOD
TO SAN BERNAR
ANAHEIM
OLIVE
ORANGE
SANTA ANA
TUSTIN
KATHRYN
VENTA
IRVINE
RANCH
IRVINE (VALENCIA)
EL TOR
Rio Hondo
Los Angeles River
San Gabriel River
Santa Ana River
HUNTINGTON BEACH
NEWPORT BEACH
LAGUNA BEACH
SERRA
DANA PT.
POCHE
SAN CLEME
PACIFIC
the Surf Line
San Diegan
Santa Fe
339
SANTA FE
220
Amtrak
Route of the San Diegans
Los Angeles
Redondo Jct.
Hobart
Rivera
Santa Fe Springs
La Mirada
Fullerton
Anaheim
Orange
Santa Ana
Venta
1.2
El Toro
.8
San Juan Capistrano
Serra
San Onofre

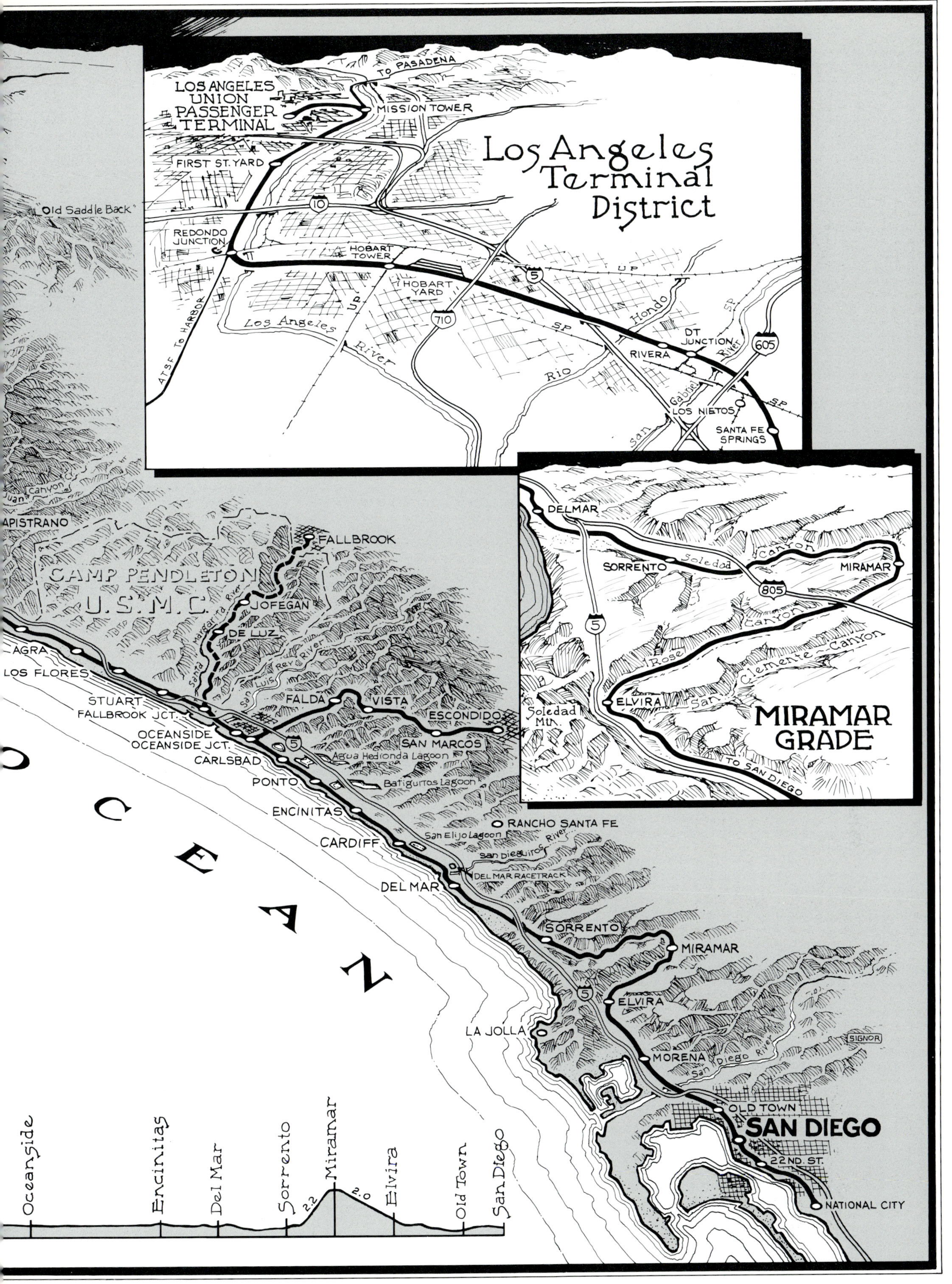

Los Angeles Terminal District
TO PASADENA
LOS ANGELES UNION PASSENGER TERMINAL
MISSION TOWER
FIRST ST. YARD
REDONDO JUNCTION
HOBART TOWER
HOBART YARD
10
5
710
605
UP
SP
Hondo
DT JUNCTION
RIVERA
Los Angeles River
Rio
San Gabriel River
LOS NIETOS
SANTA FE SPRINGS
ATSF TO HARBOR
Old Saddle Back
MIRAMAR GRADE
DELMAR
SORRENTO
Soledad Canyon
MIRAMAR
805
Rose Canyon
San Clemente Canyon
Soledad Mtn.
ELVIRA
TO SAN DIEGO
Juan Canyon
APISTRANO
FALLBROOK
CAMP PENDLETON U.S.M.C.
JOFEGAN
DE LUZ
Santa Margarita River
San Luis Rey River
AGRA
LOS FLORES
STUART
FALLBROOK JCT.
OCEANSIDE
OCEANSIDE JCT.
FALDA
VISTA
ESCONDIDO
SAN MARCOS
Agua Hedionda Lagoon
CARLSBAD
PONTO
Batiquitos Lagoon
ENCINITAS
RANCHO SANTA FE
CARDIFF
San Elijo Lagoon
San Dieguito River
DEL MAR RACETRACK
DEL MAR
OCEAN
SORRENTO
MIRAMAR
ELVIRA
LA JOLLA
MORENA
San Diego River
SIGNOR
OLD TOWN
SAN DIEGO
22ND. ST.
NATIONAL CITY
Oceanside
Encinitas
Del Mar
Sorrento
Miramar
Elvira
Old Town
San Diego
2.2
2.0

Left: One of the more interesting locations on the Surf Line is Fallbrook Junction, where for a mile the railroad is between the two halves of Interstate 5. Weekend-only No. 575 scoots along northbound on August 6, 1988. Below: As seen from the vestibule of a southbound **San Diegan,** *the 1946-built Oceanside depot was well-used in this early seventies view. This depot has since been replaced by a futuristic structure. (See color section of this book.)*
Both photos, Dick Stephenson

Just north of Oceanside is Fallbrook Junction, so named because it is the point where the old Fallbrook Branch and the original main line from San Bernardino connect. Reduced in 1978 to just a stub of its former self, the branch serves Camp Pendleton, and makes a convenient point for delivery of heavy equipment moving by rail.

Oceanside—Rail Hub

While Oceanside may appear to visitors to be almost an extension of nearby Camp Pendleton, it really serves as a hub of commerce for the entire North San Diego County area.

Oceanside also serves as a hub on the railroad. Santa Fe freight operations are directed from the newly relocated Oceanside Yard that opened in January 1988 on the northern edge of town. The Escondido Local picks up and delivers cars to this yard for shipment to San Bernardino, Barstow and beyond.

The stucco Santa Fe depot (built in 1946) was demolished in mid-1988 to make way for redevelopment of the downtown area. The Oceanside Transportation Center (opened in 1984) now serves the needs of local residents and visitors. It combines rail, and intercity and local buses in one modern facility.

Another modest concrete building was demolished on the old station site. It had housed the dispatcher's office for the Centralized Traffic Control (CTC) machine that was installed in 1944 to control the line from El Toro to San Diego. More than one fascinated young man stopped by over the years to see what the man in that little building

was doing; the lights and levers on the board controlled switches and signals up to forty miles away.

On the south edge of town, Escondido Junction marks the point at which the 21-mile line to Escondido takes off. Passenger service has been gone from this branch for over thirty years.

Mixed train service lasted on both the Escondido and Fallbrook Branches until 1948.

Along the Water's Edge

Heading south from Oceanside the line crosses seven major stream inlets in the next 20 miles. Unlike some beachfront homes, the tracks are seldom inundated. The railroad, in the 100 years that it has used this right-of-way, has figured out what elevation it needs to maintain to keep the trackage out of the water. The grade is gentle, and trains make good time here, passing through the communities of Carlsbad, Leucadia, Encinitas, Cardiff and Solana Beach. The next stop is Del Mar, an elegant and monied community nestled in hills alongside the sea. The old brick depot (built in 1910) seems to be from another era, but it continues to serve passengers today much as it has for years. The city was incorporated in 1959, and has expanded considerably in the last fifteen years.

Above: Even with eight trains per day each way, the right-of-way just south of Del Mar gets more attention from walkers and joggers than trains. Right: The Del Mar depot, built in 1910. Until recently, the agent's quarters upstairs were rented out. Below: Del Mar marks the spot where the line leaves the coast and heads up through the Sorrento Valley to tackle Miramar Hill. This view looks southeast under the old Highway 101 overpass. All three views were taken in August 1988.
Three photos, Dick Stephenson

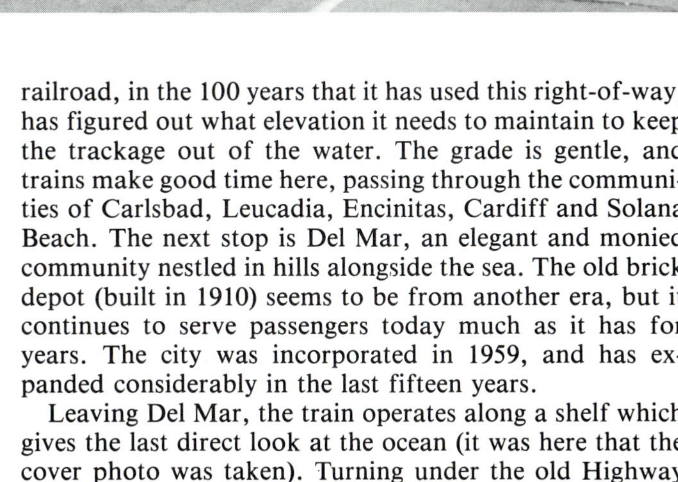

Leaving Del Mar, the train operates along a shelf which gives the last direct look at the ocean (it was here that the cover photo was taken). Turning under the old Highway 101 underpass at Torrey Pines State Reserve, the tracks shoot straight to the southeast into the Sorrento Valley. To the right are the communities of Torrey Pines and La Jolla. On the left are more examples of the continued growth in

PA No. 57 and a mate lead a four-car No. 83 past Linda Vista (later Miramar) depot on January 3, 1955, replacing the two RDC cars. This depot was an important train order office before the installation of CTC, especially for the movement of helper engines. **John Shaw**

new housing in the area, with tract after tract of new condominiums. After passing under Interstate 5 there are a number of light industrial/commercial buildings on the left in the Sorrento area.

Miramar Hill Grade

As though saving something of some substance until near the end of the ride, the line climbs out of the Sorrento Valley toward Miramar. The 2.2 percent, three-mile-long grade is substantial, with train speed slowing to twenty-five mph due to the gradient and curvature. In steam days, trains frequently had to add a second engine to pull the hill. The top of the hill is reached through a narrow cut before the upper reaches of Rose Canyon open up. Heading down the south side of the hill, train speed increases. The line is double-tracked between Miramar and Elvira. Trains often are scheduled to pass in this nearly five-mile stretch. The bottom of the canyon is narrow, and the crossing of the bridge across Rose Creek is relatively slow.

Entering the Silver Gate City

The ride still is not over, as you are just at the northern edge of the city. The tracks parallel Interstate 5 and the eastern edge of Mission Bay. After making a couple of sweeping curves near the site of old Morena siding, and heading out across the San Diego River, you find yourself at Old Town, where the line again becomes double track. Your train will keep to the left here, a remnant from the days when the train was turned around after leaving San Diego depot, and ran left-handed to Old Town.

On the right after crossing under Interstate 5 is the old Consolidated Aircraft plant, the largest on the West Coast during World War II. The tracks also pass very close to San Diego International Airport, where planes pass so low in landing that it seems that air passengers can look right into building windows.

The ever-growing skyline of San Diego reaches out to welcome arriving passengers. With the train station located right downtown, it is easy to get to locations throughout the city. Right across the street from the station, for example (at Kettner Boulevard and C Street), is the downtown terminus of the San Diego Trolley. From here you can board cars for either the East or South line, which can whisk you to the border or other destinations. Attractions such as the zoo and Sea World are short bus rides away. Seaport Village and the waterfront are within easy walking distance.

San Diego has undergone tremendous growth in the last twenty years. From a medium-sized city of about 700,000 it has grown to over one million (half the current population of the county). Major buildings dot its skyline, and the growth in both business and residential construction is seemingly endless. This city has a near-perfect climate . . . often much cooler than Los Angeles in the summer, blessed with breezes, and nearly free from smog. No wonder so many have come to visit and then stayed.

Variety and Spice

In the 128-mile trip from Los Angeles you have passed through large and small cities, viewed forty-five miles of sparkling coastline, passed through valleys and over hills. Every day thousands of passengers take advantage of all or just a part of this remarkable ride. Whether past, present or future, we hope you enjoy this experience.

Above: This high-angle view of the San Diego depot in February 1974 looks east from the Holiday Inn. Many buildings visible in this photo had disappeared by the mid-eighties, and the track layout had changed. Of note in the consist of No. 777 is an ex-ambulance car converted to a baggage-dorm. The tall building under construction is the Metropolitan Correctional Center; behind it is the bridge to Coronado. Below: Behind the depot, on C St., runs another success story in Public Transit. The San Diego Trolley, with ridership figures and farebox revenues beyond its planners' wildest dreams, runs electric cars to San Ysidro on the original (south) line. A second (east) line, to El Cajon, is well under way, with the segment to Euclid Ave. already in service. This car was about to depart for Euclid Ave. in this October 1988 view.

Dennis J. Kogan; Dick Stephenson

1951
– in Comparison

A few details ABOUT SANTA FE STREAMLINED TRAIN SERVICE BETWEEN LOS ANGELES AND SAN DIEGO.....

★ Following the Pacific Ocean Coastline, the San Diegan service offers our patrons some of the most remarkable scenery in the world. Four schedules daily each way.

These Streamliner trains carry a baggage car, modern chair cars and lounge car. Also Fred Harvey diner (except trains 78 and 79). All equipment air-conditioned.

The Santa Fe Railway takes great pleasure in presenting to you this fast Streamliner train service between Los Angeles and San Diego, California.

[signature] Passenger Traffic Manager, Los Angeles, Calif.

Enroute

Santa Fe

ABOARD THE SAN DIEGAN

A log of your trip
BETWEEN LOS ANGELES AND SAN DIEGO

LOS ANGELES ...... ★ *Alt. 318; pop. 1,954,036.* Los Angeles County has 4,116,901 inhabitants. Founded Sept. 4, 1781, as the "City of the Angels." Los Angeles was the second town to be officially incorporated (1850) in California. General Fremont raised the Stars and Stripes here in 1846. In addition to the University of California at Los Angeles, the University of Southern California and Occidental College, there are hundreds of other public schools. No other city of its size has such extensive urban and interurban railways, all electric. Los Angeles Harbor is now one of the greatest in the world. Its growth has been phenomenal, and the Santa Fe Railway has built an extension 12 miles long to make Los Angeles Harbor one of its Pacific Terminals. Hollywood, suburb of Los Angeles, is film capital of the world. Additional studios at Burbank and Culver City.

SANTA FE SPRINGS.. ★ *15 miles from Los Angeles; alt. 280; pop. 200.* Scene of sensational oil development beginning in October, 1921. At peak of oil activity population exceeded 2000. Production area amounted to 1650 acres with 500 wells. The field was one of the world's largest producers of high gravity oil.

FULLERTON .... ★ *26 miles from Los Angeles; alt. 161; pop. 14,500.* Valencia orange orchards, walnuts and oil wells. There are 22 industrial and citrus packing plants, with capital of $3,000,000. Annual output of field and orchard products over $15,000,000, utilizing 2600 employees with annual payroll of $4,785,500.

ANAHEIM .... ★ *28 miles from Los Angeles; alt. 158; pop. 14,500.* Founded 1857 by Germans from San Francisco. Industrial and citrus center of Orange County. Eight orange packing houses, six citrus by-products processing plants. Chemicals, paints and copper wire factories.

ORANGE .... ★ *33 miles from Los Angeles; alt. 172; pop. 10,053.* Citrus groves, citrus and walnut packing. Copper wire, cable, rope plants. Cotton mills, gold beating.

SANTA ANA....... ★ *36 miles from Los Angeles; alt. 135; pop. 48,080.* County seat of Orange County. Orange and lemon packing houses, manufacturing of citrus by-products. Farm machinery, woolens, china, sugar, glass products, fruit juices, jellies and jams. Bower's Museum, Botanic Gardens, excellent recreation in nearby mountains and beaches.

IRVINE .... ★ *43 miles from Los Angeles; alt. 197; pop. 7,300 (including El Toro Marine Corps Air Station).* San Joaquin Rancho of the Irvine Co. Large acreages in citrus, walnuts, avocados. Also lima and blackeye beans, sugar beets, produce. Livestock. Near Laguna and Newport beaches.

SAN JUAN CAPISTRANO ...... ★ *58 miles from Los Angeles; alt. 104; pop. 1,400.* English walnuts, barley, beans, oranges, cattle raising. Center pottery industries. San Juan Capistrano Mission, established by Father Serra in 1776, partly destroyed by earthquake in 1812, restored by Landmark Club and local priest. Three miles south is Pacific Ocean.

SAN CLEMENTE .... ★ *64 miles from Los Angeles; alt. 200; pop. 2,100.* Summer and Winter resort. Sport fishing pier, 6½ miles fine State beach. Municipal golfcourse, annual tournament of sports (Summer). Recreation facilities. Rubber manufacture and copper gift-ware plants.

OCEANSIDE .... ★ *87 miles from Los Angeles; alt. 60; pop. 13,000.* Summer and winter resort, sport fishing pier, 3 miles of finest sandy beach. Unusually mild climate. Gateway to Palomar Observatory and world's most powerful telescope. Camp Pendleton, Marine Corps base, and U. S. Naval Hospital. San Luis Rey Mission, founded 1798, 4 miles east; San Antonio del Pala Mission 25 miles; Warner's Hot Springs 50 miles east. Mt. Ecclesia, headquarters Rosicrucian Fellowship. Important vegetable growing district. Santa Fe branches to Escondido and Fallbrook.

CARLSBAD .... ★ *90 miles from Los Angeles; alt. 41; pop. 6,800.* S. D. Army and Navy Military Academy. California Carlsbad Mineral Springs Hotel. Royal Palms Inn, Twin Inns. Bulbs, flowers, fruits and vegetables. Excellent motels, restaurants and beautiful beach.

ENCINITAS .... ★ *99 miles from Los Angeles; alt. 79; pop. 6,000.* Most equable climate in U.S. Noted for picturesque beaches, salt water fishing, year-round culture of flowers, avocados and other tropical fruits.

CARDIFF .... ★ *100 miles from Los Angeles; alt. 44; pop. 1,000.* (Cardiff-by-the-Sea). Residential area, ocean bathing, fishing, sub-tropical fruits, flowers and plants.

SOLANA BEACH .... ★ *102 miles from Los Angeles; alt. 65; pop. 2,500.* Gateway for more than 20 square miles of irrigation land famous for avocados and vegetables. Scientific instruments manufactured. Public bathing beach.

DEL MAR .... ★ *105 miles from Los Angeles; alt. 123; pop. 975.* Bathing beach and fishing pier. Famous Torrey Pines. Rancho Santa Fe, country estates and site of The Inn, 5 miles. Del Mar Race Track and Rancho Santa Fe Golf Course. Luxurious Hotel Del Mar. San Diego County Fair Grounds.

LINDA VISTA ...... ★ *113 miles from Los Angeles; alt. 377;* Station for Camp Miramar.

SAN DIEGO........ ★ *128 miles from Los Angeles; alt. 13 to 822; pop. 321,485.* On San Diego Bay, discovered in 1542 by Cabrillo and named in 1602 by Viscaino. Harbor area of 22 square miles. Headquarters of 11th Naval District and home port of large part of U. S. Navy. $300,000,000 invested in Naval shore establishments. County seat of San Diego county. Site of first Mission in California, built in 1769. Across bay is city of Coronado, with famous Hotel del Coronado, and Navy's greatest aviation base at North Island. San Diego has six tuna canneries. City is built around 1400-acre Balboa Park, containing third largest zoo in world, several museums and full recreational facilities. Fine beach resorts in City include La Jolla, Pacific Beach, Mission Beach and Ocean Beach. Ample accommodations for tourists.

25M 8-2-51

This pocket-sized guide from 1951 provided some interesting information about points along the line. It is interesting to compare this with the information in Chapter 5, and to see how things have changed over the years. **Jim McClellan/Dick Stephenson Collection**

Jas. B. Duffy, Asst.Pass.Traf.Mgr., Los Angeles T.B.Gallaher,Pass.Traf.Mgr.,Chicago

SCHEDULE of TRAINS BETWEEN

Los Angeles • San Diego

CORRECTED TO JUNE 12, 1938

LOS ANGELES TO SAN DIEGO

	STATIONS	No. 72 Daily	†No. 74 Daily	No. 76 Daily	†No. 78 Daily	No. 24 Daily	No. 54 Daily
Lv	Los Angeles	9.01AM	1.00PM	3.45PM	8.30 PM	8.15AM	5.20PM
	Redondo Junction	....	....	....	....	....	f5.25
	Hobart	....	....	....	....	....	f5.30
	Bandini	....	....	....	....	....	f5.33
	Rivera	....	....	....	....	....	f5.39
	Los Nietos	....	....	....	....	....	f5.42
	Santa Fe Springs	....	....	....	....	....	5.45
	La Mirada	....	....	....	....	....	f5.51
	Buena Park	....	....	....	....	....	f5.53
	Fullerton	9 35	....	4.20	....	8.48	6.02
	Anaheim	9.41	....	4.25	....		
	Orange	9 51	....	4.32	....		
	Santa Ana	10.00	1.39	4.40	9.09		
	Venta	....	....	....	....		
	Irvine	f10.12	....	....	....		
	El Toro	f10.19	....	....	....		
	Gallvan	....	....	....	....		
	S. J. Capistrano	f10.32	....	....	....		
o	Serra	....	....	....	....		
	San Clemente	f10.42	....	f 5.16	....		
	San Onofre	f10.50	....	....	....		
	Agra	....	....	....	....		
	Las Flores	....	....	....	....		
	Stuart	....	....	....	....		
	Oceanside	11.20AM	2.37	5.50	10.07		
	Carlsbad	f11.26	....	....	....		
	Ponto	....	....	....	....		
	Encinitas	f11.40	....	....	....		
	Cardiff	f11 43	....	....	....		
	Solana Beach	f11.45	....	....	....		
	Del Mar	f11.49	▲2.56	f 6.13	▲10.26		
	Sorrento	....	....	....	....		
	Linda Vista	f12.08	....	....	....		
	Selwyn	....	....	....	....		
	Elvira	....	....	....	....		
	Ladrillo	....	....	....	....		
Ar	San Diego	12.30PM	3.30PM	6.45 PM	11.00PM		

No. 74: "THE SAN DIEGAN" — No. 78: "THE SAN DIEGAN" — No. 54: MOTOR

Nos. 72 and 76 will stop at any station to discharge revenue passengers from east or north of Barstow or Santa Barbara or north.

Parlor cars run on trains 72, 74, 76 and 78 Los Angeles to San Diego. o Doheny Park.
▲ Stop to discharge revenue passengers from Los Angeles and Santa Ana.

No. 72 will stop at Los Nietos and La Mirada to pick up revenue passengers destined San Diego. Nos. 72-76 will stop at Carlsbad to discharge revenue passengers from Los Angeles. † All seats on Nos. 74 and 78, both Coach and Parlor Car, are reserved. f Flag stop.

★ LOS ANGE[illegible] DIEGO

	STATIONS	No. 70 Daily	No. 72 Daily	No. 74 Daily	No. 76 Daily	No. 7[illegible] Daily	[illegible]24 Daily	No. 54 Daily
Lv	Los Angeles	AM 8.30	AM 9.30	PM 12.30	PM 4.00	PM 9.10	AM 8.00	PM 5.20
	Redondo Junction		....				....	f 5.29
	Hobart		....				....	....
	Bandini		....				....	f5.37
	Rivera		....				....	f5.40
	Los Nietos		●9.52				....	f5.42
	Santa Fe Springs		....				....	5.45
	La Mirada		....				....	f5.50
	Buena Park		....				....	f5.53
	Fullerton		10.05				Ar 8.33	Ar 5.58
	Anaheim		10.15				....	
	Orange		10.25				....	
	Santa Ana	9.17	10.33	1.15	4.45	9.55	....	
	Venta	....		....	....	....	....	
	Irvine		f10.43		....		....	
	El Toro		f10.50		....		....	
	Gallvan		....		....		....	
	S. J. Capistrano		f11.00		....		....	
o	Serra		f11.05		....		....	
	San Clemente		f11.11		....		....	
	San Onofre		f11.18		....		....	
	Agra		....		....		....	
	Las Flores	....	....	....	....	....	....	
	Stuart	....	....	....	....	....	....	
	Oceanside	10.18	11.45	2.15	5.45	10.55	....	
	Carlsbad	....	f11.53	....	....	....	....	
	Ponto	....	....	....	....	....	....	
	Encinitas	....	f12.06	....	....	....	....	
	Cardiff	....	f12.10	....	....	....	....	
	Solana Beach	....	f12.14	....	....	....	....	
•	Del Mar	▲10.37	f12.20	▲2.37	▲6.07	▲11.17	....	
	Sorrento	....	f12.28	....	....	....	....	
	Linda Vista	....	f12.39	....	....	....	....	
	Selwyn	....	....	....	....	....	....	
	Elvira	....	....	....	....	....	....	
	Ladrillo	....	....	....	....	....	....	
Ar	San Diego	AM 11.15	PM 1.10	PM 3.15	PM 6.45	PM 11.55	....	

No. 70: Chair Cars, Parlor-Lounge Car, Fred Harvey Diner; "THE SAN DIEGAN" — No. 72: (SEE Note) — No. 74: Chair Cars, Parlor-Lounge Car, Fred Harvey Diner; "THE SAN DIEGAN" — No. 76: Chair Cars, Parlor-Lounge Car, Fred Harvey Diner; "THE SAN DIEGAN" — No. 78: Chair Cars, Parlor-Lounge Car, Fred Harvey Diner; "THE SAN DIEGAN" — No. 54: MOTOR

▲ Nos. 70-74-76-78 stop to discharge revenue passengers from Los Angeles, Santa Ana.
● Doheny Park.

Note: Chair Cars, Cafe-Observation Car.
● No. 72 will stop at Los Nietos to pick up revenue passengers destined San Diego. No. 72 will stop at any station to discharge passengers from points east or north of Barstow and Southern Pacific points Santa Barbara or north. f Flag stop.

• Rancho Santa Fe.

"SAN DIEGANS" CARRY PARLOR-LOUNGE AND FRED HARVEY DINER

Timetables changed little over the years. These from 1938 (left), 1942 (above), and 1955 (below) carry explicit notes about flag stops and other restrictions, plus information about other services such as parlor and dining. The front cover from these and other selected dates are at top left and bottom right. **Brian Norden Collection; Dick Stephenson Collection; Dennis Ryan Collection**

★ LOS ANGELES to SAN DIEGO

	STATIONS Pac. Standard Time	No. 72 Daily	No. 80 Daily	No. 74 Daily	No. 76 Daily	No. 82 Daily	No. 78 Daily	No. 70 Daily
Lv	Los Angeles	AM 7.45	AM 10.00	PM 12 30	PM 3.30	PM 5.30	PM 8 00	PM 11 20
	First Street							
	Hobart							
	Bandini							
	Rivera	▲8.01		▲12 46	▲3 46			
	Los Nietos							
	Santa Fe Springs							
	La Mirada							f 11.46
	Buena Park							
	Fullerton	8.15	10 29	1 01	4 00	6 00	8.30	11.55
	Anaheim		f10.32			f 6 05		12.04
	Orange		f10.37			f 6 12		12.11
	Santa Ana	8.30	10.42	1 15	4 15	6 20	8 45	12.20
	Irvine							f12.32
	El Toro							f12.40
	San Juan Capistrano		f11.01			f 6 39		f12.55
⊕	Serra							f 1.01
	San Clemente		f11.08		f4 41	f 6 47	f9 11	f 1.09
	San Onofre							f 1.17
	Oceanside	9.20	11.28	2.00	5 05	7.08	9.35	1.50
	Carlsbad							f 2.00
	Encinitas		f11.40			f 7 20	f9.47	f 2.15
	Cardiff							f 2.20
	Solana Beach							f 2.25
:	Del Mar	9.38	11.48	2 20	5 23	7 26	9 54	2.35
	Sorrento							f 2.48
	Linda Vista							f 3.00
Ar	San Diego	AM 10.15	PM 12 30	PM 3 00	PM 6.00	PM 8 05	PM 10 30	AM 3.45

No. 72: Chair Cars — Club-Lounge; "THE SAN DIEGAN" — No. 80: Rail Diesel Chair Cars — No. 74: Chair Cars — Club-Lounge; "THE SAN DIEGAN" — No. 76: Chair Cars — Club-Lounge; "THE SAN DIEGAN" — No. 82: Rail Diesel Chair Cars — No. 78: Chair Cars Club-Lounge; "THE SAN DIEGAN" — No. 70: (Chair Cars Only)

f. Flag stop to pick up or discharge revenue passengers.
No baggage carried to Linda Vista.
: Rancho Santa Fe and La Jolla.
▲ Stops to pick up passengers for Oceanside, Del Mar, and San Diego.
⊕ Doheny Park

RESERVED SEATS AVAILABLE at a slight additional charge on trains 72, 74, 76, 78.
The Atchison, Topeka and Santa Fe Ry. Co. will not be responsible for errors in these time tables nor for inconvenience or damage resulting from delayed trains or failure to make connections. Dark face indicates P.M.—Light face A.M.

ALL SCHEDULES PACIFIC STANDARD TIME

★ SAN DIEGO to LOS ANGELES

	STATIONS Pac. Standard Time	No. 81 Daily	No. 71 Daily	No. 73 Daily	No. 75 Daily	No. 83 Daily	No. 77 Daily	No. 79 Daily
Lv	San Diego	AM 7.00	AM 9.00	AM 11.45	PM 1.00	PM 2.00	PM 4.00	PM 8.00
	Linda Vista				f 1 23			
	Sorrento				f 1 29			
:	Del Mar	7.29	9.29	12 14	1 35	2 29	4 29	8 29
	Solana Beach				f 1 38			
	Cardiff				f 1 41			
	Encinitas	f 7.35	f 9.35		f 1 45	f 2 35		
	Carlsbad				f 1 55			
Ar	Oceanside	7.47	9.47	12 32	2 20	2 47	4 47	8 47
	San Onofre				f 2 47			
	San Clemente	f 8.05	f10.05		f 2 53	f 3.05		f 9 05
⊕	Serra				f 3 00			
	S. J. Capistrano	f 8.12			f 3 05	f 3 12		
	El Toro				f 3 30			
	Irvine				f 3 36			
	Santa Ana	8.32	10 34	1 23	3 55	3 32	5 42	9 38
	Orange	f 8.37			4 05	f 3 37		
	Anaheim	f 8.44			f 4 15	f 3 44		
Lv	Fullerton	8.47	▲10.50	1.35	4 30	3 48	5.55	9.50
Lv	Buena Park							
	La Mirada				f4 40			
	Santa Fe Springs							
	Los Nietos							
	Rivera		▲11.04	▲1.50			▲6.09	▲10.04
	Bandini							
	Hobart							
	Redondo Junction							
	First Street							
Ar	Los Angeles	AM 9.30	AM 11.30	PM 2 15	PM 5 30	PM 4 30	PM 6 35	PM 10 30

No. 81: Rail Diesel Chair Cars — No. 71: Chair Cars — Club-Lounge; "THE SAN DIEGAN" — No. 73: Chair Cars Club-Lounge; "THE SAN DIEGAN" — No. 75: (Chair Cars Only) — No. 83: Rail Diesel Chair Cars — No. 77: Chair Cars Club-Lounge; "THE SAN DIEGAN" — No. 79: Chair Cars — Club-Lounge; "THE SAN DIEGAN"

f. Flag stop to pick up or discharge revenue passengers.
▲ Stops to discharge passengers from San Diego, Del Mar, and Oceanside.
: Rancho Santa Fe and La Jolla.
⊕ Doheny Park

RESERVED SEATS AVAILABLE AT A SLIGHT ADDITIONAL CHARGE ON TRAINS 71, 73, 77, 79.

ALL SCHEDULES PACIFIC STANDARD TIME

SAN DIEGAN STREAMLINERS between LOS ANGELES — SAN DIEGO

All Schedules Pacific Standard Time

ADD ONE HOUR FOR CALIFORNIA DAYLIGHT SAVING TIME

PAGE 2

Dark face figures indicate P.M. time; light type A.M.

STATIONS	No. 70 Daily	No. 72 Daily	No. 74 Daily	No. 76 Daily	No. 78 Daily	§No. 80 Sun. and Holidays only
Pacific Standard Time	AM	AM	AM	PM	PM	PM
Lv Los Angeles	12.45	6.05	9.20	1.30	4.45	8.15
Pico Rivera		a 6.21	a 9.42	a 1.52	a 5.07	
Fullerton	1.29	6.40	10.00	2.10	5.25	8.51
Anaheim	f 1.35	f 6.45	J 10.05		f 5.30	
Orange	f 1.42	f 6.52	J 10.12			
Santa Ana	1.54	7.05	10.24	2.29	5.45	9.10
Irvine						
El Toro						
San Juan Capistrano		f 7.23	J 10.43	b 2.47	b 6.09	
San Clemente	2.30	f 7.33	f 10.53	b 2.57	f 6.18	b 9.37
Oceanside	3.00	8.00	11.22	3.25	6.42	10.00
Encinitas	f 3.14				f 6.54	
†Del Mar	3.20	8.25	11.42	3.49	7.04	10.20
Ar San Diego	4.00	9.00	12.15	4.25	7.40	10.55
	AM	AM	PM	PM	PM	PM

f. Flag stop to pick up or discharge revenue passengers.
g. To receive passengers for Los Angeles or discharge passengers from Oceanside and beyond.
a. Stops to pick up or discharge to or from Oceanside and beyond.
b. Stops to pick up or discharge passengers to or from Los Angeles.
† Rancho Santa Fe and La Jolla.

STATIONS	*No. 71 Daily exc. Sun. and Holidays	No. 73 Daily	No. 75 Daily	No. 77 Daily	§No. 79 Sun. and Holidays only	No. 81 Daily
Pacific Standard Time	AM	AM	AM	PM	PM	PM
Lv San Diego	5.05	6.50	11.50	4.15	6.00	8.00
†Del Mar	5.35	7.21	12.23	4.48	6.30	8.30
Encinitas	b 5.42	f 7.27	b 12.29	b 4.54		
Oceanside	5.55	7.45	12.47	5.12	6.50	8.55
San Clemente	f 6.14	f 8.08	1.09	5.33		9.20
San Juan Capistrano	6.22					
El Toro						
Irvine						
Santa Ana	6.42	8.42	1.45	6.09	7.40	9.53
Orange		g 8.47		b 6.14		
Anaheim	f 6.55	f 8.54		f 6.20		
Fullerton	7.02	9.02	2.02	6.27	8.00	10.10
Pico Rivera	a 7.17	a 9.17	a 2.17	a 6.42	a 8.15	a 10.25
Ar Los Angeles	7.45	9.45	2.45	7.10	8.40	10.50
	AM	AM	PM	PM	PM	PM

j. Stops to discharge passengers from San Bernardino and beyond.
* Operated daily except Sundays and New Year's Day, Washington's Birthday, Memorial Day, Independence Day, Labor Day, Thanksgiving Day and Christmas Day.
§ Operated Sundays, New Year's Day, Washington's Birthday, Memorial Day, Independence Day, Labor Day, Thanksgiving Day and Christmas Day.

For Train Information, Phone

SAN FRA... SUtter 1-7600
...ison 4-0171
...t 2-2961
...ES:
...irectory

No. 124 Daily	STATIONS		No. 123 Daily
1.45 PM	Lv Los Angeles	Ar	12.10 PM
▽	Pico-Rivera		▽
2.28	Fullerton		11.23
2.47	Corona (Norco)		f 10.50
3.15	Riverside		10.25
3.40	Ar San Bernardino	Lv	10.00 AM

▽ Denotes conditional stop to pick up or discharge passengers to or from Williams Jct., Arizona and beyond.

The SUPER CHIEF

Lv. San Diego . . . 4:15 p.m.
via the San Diegan

Lv. Los Angeles . . 8:00 p.m.
via the SUPER CHIEF

Ar. Chicago . . . . 1:30 p.m.
(two nights enroute)

SANTA FE RAIL-BUS
Co-ordinated Schedules

SAN FRANCISCO-LOS ANGELES-SAN DIEGO

SAN FRANCISCO
OAKLAND
BERKELEY
RICHMOND
PITTSBURG
STOCKTON
EMPIRE
MERCED
FRESNO
HANFORD
BAKERSFIELD
PASADENA
LOS ANGELES
FULLERTON
SANTA ANA
OCEANSIDE
DEL MAR
SAN DIEGO

SANTA FE

April 29, 1962

Santa Fe

Santa Fe Railway Company

Local California Time Tables

TIMES SHOWN
PACIFIC STANDARD TIME

October 30, 1966

Santa Fe Railway Co.

SAN DIEGAN STREAMLINERS

LOS ANGELES — SAN DIEGO

Santa Fe

Santa Fe

Dark type figures indicate P.M. time; light type A.M.

STATIONS	No. 74 Daily	No. 76 Daily	No. 78 Daily
	AM	AM	PM
Lv Los Angeles	7.30	11.00	7.45
Pico Rivera	a 7.48	a 11.22	a 8.07
Fullerton	8.05	11.40	8.25
Anaheim	8.10	11.45	8.30
Orange	b 8.17	d 11.50	.....
Santa Ana	8.30	11.59	8.45
San Juan Capistrano	b 8.48	d 12.17	b 9.09
San Clemente	f 8.59	b 12.27	f 9.18
Oceanside	9.25	12.55	9.42
Encinitas	b 9.35	b 1.06	f 9.54
Del Mar, Rancho Santa Fe & La Jolla	9.45	1.19	10.04
Ar San Diego	10.25	1.55	10.40
	AM	PM	PM

STATIONS	No. 73 Daily	No. 75 Daily	No. 77 Daily
	AM	AM	PM
Lv San Diego	7.00	11.30	4.00
Del Mar, Rancho Santa Fe & La Jolla	7.31	12.03	4.33
Encinitas	f 7.37	b 12.09	b 4.39
Oceanside	7.55	12.27	4.57
San Clemente	f 8.17	12.48	5.18
San Juan Capistrano	b 8.27	.....	.....
Santa Ana	8.52	1.25	5.54
Orange	c 8.57	.....	b 5.59
Anaheim	9.04	1.35	6.05
Fullerton	9.12	1.42	6.12
Pico Rivera	a 9.30	a 2.00	a 6.30
Ar Los Angeles	9.55	2.25	6.55
	AM	PM	PM

a. Stops to pick up or discharge passengers to or from Oceanside and beyond.
b. Stops to pick up or discharge passengers to of from Los Angeles.
c. To receive passengers for Los Angeles or discharge passengers from Oceanside and beyond.
d. Stops to discharge passengers from San Bernardino and beyond.
f. Flag stop to pick up or discharge revenue passengers.

Co.

...ERS

Santa Fe

No. 78 Daily
PM
8.30
a 8.52
9.10
9.15
.....
9.30
9.48
f 9.57
10.21
f 10.30
10.40
11.15
PM

No. 77 Daily
PM
4.00
4.33
b 4.39
4.57
5.18
5.27
5.54
b 5.59
6.05
6.12
a 6.30
6.55
PM

a. Stops to pick up or discharge passengers to or from Oceanside and beyond.
b. Stops to pick up or discharge passengers to or from Los Angeles.
c. To receive passengers for Los Angeles or discharge passengers from Oceanside and beyond.
d. Stops to discharge passengers from San Bernardino and beyond.
f. Flag stop to pick up or discharge revenue passengers.

*Local timetables have been pocket-sized for some time. At top is the **San Diegan** portion of the April 29, 1962, schedule, while at right is one from November 29, 1967, overlaid on the last Santa Fe schedule, from September 13, 1970.*

Dick Stephenson Collection

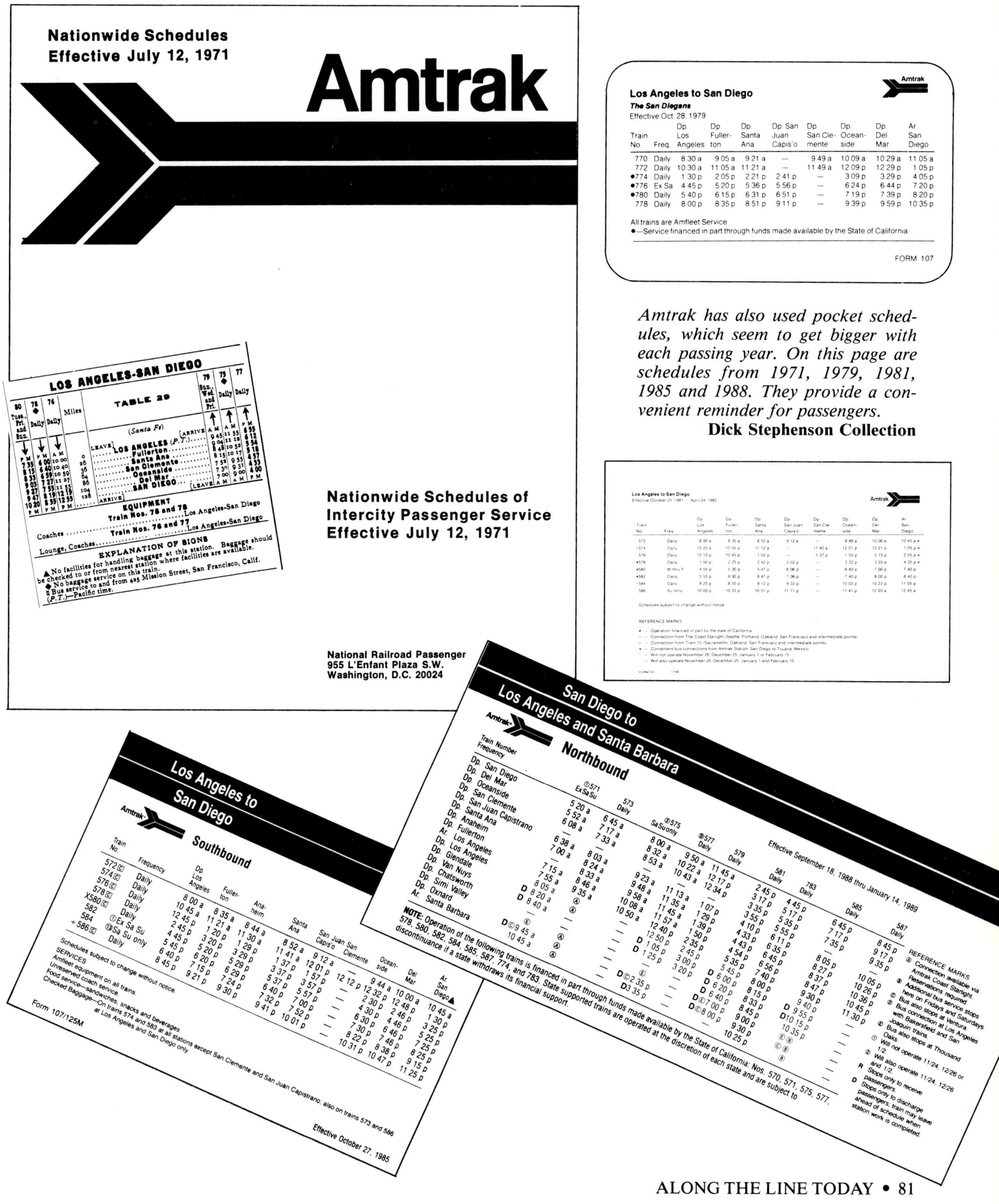

Nationwide Schedules
Effective July 12, 1971

Amtrak

LOS ANGELES-SAN DIEGO

TABLE 29

80 Tues., Fri. and Sun.	78 ◆ Daily	76 Daily	Miles	(Santa Fe)	79 Sun., Wed. and Fri.	75 ◆ Daily	77 Daily
P M 7 35	P M 6 00	A M 10 00	0	LEAVE ......LOS ANGELES (P.T.)......ARRIVE	A M 9 45	A M 11 55	P M 6 55
8 15	6 40	10 40	26	........Fullerton........	9 04	11 18	6 12
8 33	6 59	10 59	36	........Santa Ana........	8 48	10 59	5 54
9 03	7 27	11 27	64	........San Clemente........	8 15	10 17	5 18
9 27	7 55	11 55	86	........Oceanside........	7 59	9 55	4 57
9 47	8 19	12 19	104	........Del Mar........	7 39	9 31	4 33
10 20	8 55	12 55	128	ARRIVE ......SAN DIEGO......LEAVE	7 00	9 00	4 00
P M	P M	P M			A M	A M	P M

EQUIPMENT
Train Nos. 75 and 78
Coaches ....Los Angeles-San Diego
Train Nos. 76 and 77
Lounge, Coaches..........................Los Angeles-San Diego

EXPLANATION OF SIGNS
▲ No facilities for handling baggage at this station. Baggage should be checked to or from nearest station where facilities are available.
◆ No baggage service on this train.
Ⓑ Bus service to and from 425 Mission Street, San Francisco, Calif.
(P.T.)—Pacific time.

Nationwide Schedules of Intercity Passenger Service Effective July 12, 1971

National Railroad Passenger
955 L'Enfant Plaza S.W.
Washington, D.C. 20024

Los Angeles to San Diego
The San Diegans
Effective Oct. 28, 1979

Amtrak

Train No.	Freq.	Dp. Los Angeles	Dp. Fuller-ton	Dp. Santa Ana	Dp. San Juan Capis'o	Dp. San Cle-mente	Dp. Ocean-side	Dp. Del Mar	Ar. San Diego
770	Daily	8 30 a	9 05 a	9 21 a	—	9 49 a	10 09 a	10 29 a	11 05 a
772	Daily	10 30 a	11 05 a	11 21 a	—	11 49 a	12 09 p	12 29 p	1 05 p
•774	Daily	1 30 p	2 05 p	2 21 p	2 41 p	—	3 09 p	3 29 p	4 05 p
•776	Ex Sa	4 45 p	5 20 p	5 36 p	5 56 p	—	6 24 p	6 44 p	7 20 p
•780	Daily	5 40 p	6 15 p	6 31 p	6 51 p	—	7 19 p	7 39 p	8 20 p
778	Daily	8 00 p	8 35 p	8 51 p	9 11 p	—	9 39 p	9 59 p	10 35 p

All trains are Amfleet Service
•—Service financed in part through funds made available by the State of California

FORM 107

Amtrak has also used pocket schedules, which seem to get bigger with each passing year. On this page are schedules from 1971, 1979, 1981, 1985 and 1988. They provide a convenient reminder for passengers.
Dick Stephenson Collection

Los Angeles to San Diego
Effective October 25, 1981 — April 24, 1982

Amtrak

Train No.	Freq.	Dp Los Angeles	Dp Fuller-ton	Dp Santa Ana	Dp San Juan Capis'o	Dp San Cle-mente	Dp Ocean-side	Dp Del Mar	Ar San Diego
572	Daily	8 00 a	8 35 a	8 52 a	9 12 a	—	9 46 a	10 06 a	10 45 a •
•574	Daily	10 20 a	10 55 a	11 12 a	—	11 40 a	12 01 p	12 21 p	1 05 p •
576	Daily	12 10 p	12 45 p	1 02 p	—	1 37 p	1 55 p	2 15 p	2 55 p •
•578	Daily	1 50 p	2 25 p	2 42 p	3 02 p	—	3 32 p	3 55 p	4 35 p •
•580	M thru F	4 55 p	5 30 p	5 47 p	6 06 p	—	6 40 p	7 00 p	7 40 p
•582	Daily	5 55 p	6 30 p	6 47 p	7 06 p	—	7 40 p	8 00 p	8 40 p
•584	Daily	8 20 p	8 55 p	9 12 p	9 33 p	—	10 03 p	10 23 p	11 05 p
586	Su only	10 00 p	10 33 p	10 51 p	11 11 p	—	11 41 p	12 03 a	12 45 a

Schedules subject to change without notice

REFERENCE MARKS
• — Operation financed in part by the state of California
• — Connection from The Coast Starlight (Seattle, Portland, Oakland, San Francisco and intermediate points)
• — Connection from Train 15 (Sacramento, Oakland, San Francisco and intermediate points)
• — Convenient bus connections from Amtrak Station, San Diego to Tijuana, Mexico
' — Will not operate November 26, December 25, January 1 or February 15
— Will also operate November 26, December 25, January 1 and February 15

FORM 107 175M

Los Angeles to San Diego

Amtrak

Southbound

Train No.	Frequency	Dp. Los Angeles	Fuller-ton	Ana-heim	Santa Ana	San Juan Capis'o	San Clemente	Ocean-side	Del Mar	Ar. San Diego ▲
572©	Daily	8 00 a	8 35 a	8 44 a	8 52 a	9 12 a	—	9 44 a	10 00 a	10 45 a
574©	Daily	10 45 a	11 21 a	11 30 a	11 41 a	12 01 p	12 12 p	12 32 p	12 48 p	1 30 p
576©	Daily	12 45 p	1 20 p	1 29 p	1 37 p	1 57 p	—	2 30 p	2 46 p	3 25 p
578©	Daily	2 45 p	3 20 p	3 29 p	3 37 p	3 57 p	—	4 30 p	4 46 p	5 25 p
X580©	Daily	4 45 p	5 20 p	5 29 p	5 37 p	5 57 p	—	6 30 p	6 46 p	7 25 p
582	①Ex Sa Su	5 45 p	6 20 p	6 29 p	6 40 p	7 00 p	—	7 30 p	7 46 p	8 25 p
584	⑬Sa Su only	6 40 p	7 15 p	7 24 p	7 32 p	7 52 p	—	8 22 p	8 38 p	9 15 p
+ 586©	Daily	8 45 p	9 21 p	9 30 p	9 41 p	10 01 p	—	10 31 p	10 47 p	11 25 p

Schedules subject to change without notice.
SERVICES
Amfleet equipment on all trains.
Unreserved coach service.
Food service—sandwiches, snacks and beverages.
Checked Baggage—On trains 574 and 583 at all stations except San Clemente and San Juan Capistrano; also on trains 573 and 586 at Los Angeles and San Diego only.

Form 107/125M

Effective October 27, 1985

San Diego to Los Angeles and Santa Barbara

Amtrak

Northbound

Effective September 18, 1988 thru January 14, 1989

Train Number / Frequency	①571 ExSaSu	573 Daily	②575 SaSu only	Ⓑ577 Daily	579 Daily	581 Daily	783 Daily	585 Daily	587 Daily
Dp. San Diego	5 20 a	6 45 a	8 00 a	9 50 a	11 45 a	2 45 p	4 45 p	6 45 p	8 45 p
Dp. Del Mar	5 52 a	7 17 a	8 32 a	10 22 a	12 17 p	3 17 p	5 17 p	7 17 p	9 17 p
Dp. Oceanside	6 08 a	7 33 a	8 53 a	10 43 a	12 34 p	3 35 p	5 35 p	7 35 p	9 35 p
Dp. San Clemente	—	—	—	—	—	3 55 p	5 55 p	—	—
Dp. San Juan Capistrano	6 38 a	8 03 a	9 23 a	11 13 a	1 07 p	4 10 p	6 11 p	8 05 p	10 05 p
Dp. Santa Ana	7 00 a	8 24 a	9 48 a	11 35 a	1 29 p	4 33 p	6 35 p	8 27 p	10 26 p
Dp. Anaheim	—	8 33 a	9 58 a	11 45 a	1 39 p	4 43 p	6 45 p	8 37 p	10 36 p
Dp. Fullerton	7 15 a	8 46 a	10 08 a	11 57 a	1 50 p	4 54 p	6 56 p	8 47 p	10 45 p
Ar. Los Angeles	7 55 a	9 35 a	10 50 a	12 40 p	2 35 p	5 35 p	7 40 p	9 30 p	11 30 p
Dp. Los Angeles	8 05 a	Ⓐ	—	12 50 p	2 45 p	5 45 p	8 00 p	9 40 p	—
Dp. Glendale	D 8 20 a	Ⓐ	—	D 1 05 p	3 00 p	D 6 00 p	8 15 p	D 9 55 p	—
Dp. Van Nuys	D 8 40 a	—	—	D 1 25 p	3 20 p	D 6 20 p	8 33 p	D 10 15 p	—
Dp. Chatsworth	—	—	—	—	—	D 6 40 p	8 45 p	10 35 p	—
Dp. Simi Valley	Ⓔ	Ⓐ	—	Ⓔ	—	DⒺ 7 00 p	9 00 p	Ⓔ Ⓑ	—
Dp. Oxnard	D© 9 45 a	Ⓐ	—	D© 2 35 p	—	D© 8 00 p	9 30 p	© Ⓑ	—
Ar. Santa Barbara	10 45 a	Ⓐ	—	D 3 35 p	—	—	10 25 p	Ⓑ	—

NOTE: Operation of the following trains is financed in part through funds made available by the State of California: Nos. 570, 571, 575, 577, 578, 580, 582, 584, 585, 587, 774, and 783. State supported trains are operated at the discretion of each state and are subject to discontinuance if a state withdraws its financial support.

REFERENCE MARKS
Ⓐ Connection available via Amtrak Coast Starlight.
Ⓑ Reservations required.
Ⓑ Additional bus service stops here on Fridays and Saturdays.
© Bus also stops at Ventura.
Ⓓ Bus connection at Los Angeles with Bakersfield and San Joaquin trains.
Ⓔ Bus also stops at Thousand Oaks.
① Will not operate 11/24, 12/26 or 1/2.
② Will also operate 11/24, 12/26 and 1/2.
R Stops only to receive passengers.
D Stops only to discharge passengers, train may leave ahead of schedule when station work is completed.

77	75	73	71	Ruling Grade Descending—Feet Per Mile	TIME TABLE NO. 4 October 31, 1976 — STATIONS	Mile Post	Ruling Grade Descending—Feet Per Mile	Communications Turn Tables and Wyes	Capacity of Sidings in Feet	70	72	74	76
WESTWARD FIRST CLASS										EASTWARD FIRST CLASS			
Leave Daily	Leave Daily	Leave Daily	Leave Daily							Arrive Daily	Arrive Daily	Arrive Daily	Arrive Daily
				26.4	NATIONAL CITY YL	273.1	24.3	Y	Yard				
				0.0	—3.8— 22ND STREET YL	269.3	22.7	C-R					
PM	PM	PM	AM							AM	PM	PM	PM
8.20	4.30	1.00	7.00	31.0	—1.8— SAN DIEGO YL (ABS; D.T.)	267.5	52.8	Y	Yard	s11.05	s 1.05	s 6.45	s10.55
8.27	4.37	1.07	7.07	51.7	—3.3— OLD TOWN YL	264.2	65.5			10.50	12.50	6.30	10.40
				0.0	—6.3— ELVIRA (2 TRKS.)	257.9	113.5						
				116.2	—4.9— MIRAMAR	253.0	0.0	Y					
				58.1	—3.9— SORRENTO	249.1	56.0		4877				
s 8.50	s 5.00	s 1.30	s 7.30	63.4	—5.0— DEL MAR	244.0	52.8			s10.29	s12.29	s 6.09	s10.19
				63.4	—6.0— ENCINITAS	238.1	63.4						
				64.4	—4.2— PONTO	233.8	69.7		5333				
				15.8	—6.5— ESCONDIDO JCT.	227.2	7.4	Y					
s 9.11	s 5.21	s 1.51	s 7.51	65.5	—1.0— OCEANSIDE	226.2	64.9	C-R	6096	s10.09	s12.09 PM	s 5.49	s 9.59
				69.0	—2.1— FALLBROOK JCT.	224.1	64.9	Y	4569				
				58.1	—14.9— SAN ONOFRE (TCS ATS)	209.2	26.4		4927				
	s 5.42	s 2.12		26.5	—4.4— SAN CLEMENTE	204.8	26.4			s 9.49	s11.49		
				0.0	—5.0— SERRA	199.8	60.5		4956				
s 9.40			f 8.20	0.0	—2.6— SAN JUAN CAPISTRANO	197.2	65.5					s 5.21	f 9.31
				73.9	—4.6— GALIVAN	192.6	67.3		4972				
				70.2	—4.5— EL TORO	188.1	0.0						
				63.4	—5.2— VALENCIA	182.9	22.0		5982				
				0.0	—4.4— IRVINE (2 TRKS.)	178.5	38.5	Y					
s10.02	s 6.12	s 2.42	s 8.42	14.3	—2.9— SANTA ANA	175.5	32.6	C-R	6048	s 9.21	s11.21	s 5.01	s 9.11
				39.2	—2.9— ORANGE	172.6	29.6	Y	6250				
				16.9	—4.8— S. P. Crossing ANAHEIM	167.8	22.7		3044				
s10.20 PM	s 6.30 PM	s 3.00 PM	s 9.00 AM		—2.8— FULLERTON	165.0		C-R		9.05 AM	11.05 AM	4.45 PM	8.55 PM
Arrive Daily	Arrive Daily	Arrive Daily	Arrive Daily		(107.7)					Leave Daily	Leave Daily	Leave Daily	Leave Daily
(51.0)	(51.0)	(51.0)	(51.0)		Average speed per hour					(51.0)	(51.0)	(51.0)	(51.0)

77	75	73	71	Ruling Grade	STATIONS	Mile Post	Ruling Grade	Communications	Capacity	70	72	74	76
				52.8	SAN BERNARDINO (3 TRKS.)	0.0	64.4	C-R-Y	Yard				
				52.8	—2.4— RANA	1.6	0.0						
				59.8	—1.3— COLTON S. P. Crossing (2 TRACKS)	2.9	34.8	C	Yard				
				52.8	—3.8— HIGHGROVE	6.7	7.4	B	Yard				
				14.2	—2.5— S. P. Crossing RIVERSIDE JCT.	9.2	0.0	C-R					
				52.8	—0.6— RIVERSIDE	9.8	63.4		Yard				
				52.8	—4.2— CASA BLANCA	14.0	21.1	Y	4934				
				52.8	—2.4— ARLINGTON	16.4	0.0		3095				
				52.8	—3.8— MAY	20.2	0.0		4692				
				30.1	—2.6— PORPHYRY	22.8	0.0	Y	8059				
				52.8	—1.3— CORONA	24.1	24.3	C-R	8370				
				52.8	—5.1— PRADO DAM	29.2	21.1		4735				
				52.8	—7.2— ESPERANZA	36.4	0.0		6359				
				42.2	—4.2— ATWOOD (TCS)	40.6	13.2	Y					
				42.2	—2.4— PLACENTIA	43.0	0.0						
PM	PM	PM	AM							AM	AM	PM	PM
10.20	6.30	3.00	9.00	33.4	—3.0— FULLERTON U. P. Crossing	165.0	26.9	C-R		s 9.05	s11.05	s 4.45	s 8.55
				9.2	—6.3— LA MIRADA	158.7	37.0		Yard				
				17.6	—4.3— SANTA FE SPRINGS	154.4	23.2		4300				
				26.9	—1.3— LOS NIETOS S. P. Crossing (2 TRACKS)	153.1	17.4						
				0.0	—1.0— D. T. JUNCTION S. P. Crossing	152.1	4.2						
				0.0	—0.9— PICO RIVERA	151.2	22.7	R	Yard				
				52.8	—1.4— BANDINI	149.8	22.7						
				0.0	—4.3— HOBART U. P. Crossing	145.5	37.0	C-R	Yard				
				0.0	—2.3— REDONDO JCT. U. P. Crossing	143.2	37.0	R-T-Y					
				0.0	—2.1— FIRST STREET (70.7)	141.1	59.7		Yard				
				31.7	—1.1— MISSION TOWER	140.0	71.8	C-R-Y		8.33	10.33	4.13	8.23
10.55 PM	7.05 PM	3.35 PM	9.35 AM		—0.8— LOS ANGELES Union Station					8.30 AM	10.30 AM	4.10 PM	8.20 PM
Arrive Daily	Arrive Daily	Arrive Daily	Arrive Daily		WEST (72.6) (71.6) EAST					Leave Daily	Leave Daily	Leave Daily	Leave Daily
(44.2)	(44.2)	(44.2)	(44.2)		Average speed per hour					(44.2)	(44.2)	(44.2)	(44.2)

A railroader's-eye view of the line is provided by this copy of Santa Fe's Los Angeles Division employee timetable from October 1976, which combines the two subdivisions that cover the line. With the current level of eight trains per day, this same information would not fit on this page.

Dick Stephenson Collection

Another Superb

Super Chief

The Super Chief is the only extra-fare, streamlined, 39 3/4 hour train between Chicago and California, equipped and reserved entirely for first-class passengers.

The first streamlined Super Chief was placed in service May 12, 1937, on a once-a-week round trip schedule. Its popularity was immediate and spontaneous, and it has since been booked to capacity, in season and out. Hence our pleasure in announcing the doubling of this supremely swift, luxurious and convenient service. *Commencing February 22, 1938,* the Super Chief will leave Chicago twice each week, on Tuesdays and Saturdays at 7:15 P. M.; arrive Los Angeles Thursdays and Mondays at 9:00 A. M. Eastbound, departures from Los Angeles will be Tuesdays and Fridays at 8:00 P. M., arrival Chicago at 1:45 P. M. Thursdays and Sundays.

- This new Super Chief consists of nine cars, streamlined in stainless steel behind a 3600 H. P. Diesel-electric locomotive. It presents Fred Harvey service in its dining car, cocktail-lounge car, and baggage-club car. Accommodations include drawing rooms, compartments and bed rooms, for use singly or en suite; the new roomettes, economical and comfortable, and open sections.
- The second Super Chief is a fit companion to the first, heretofore considered by many the most beautiful train on American rails.

The Chicagoan
and
The Kansas Cityan

Still they come! Chicago and Kansas City, also, are soon to have their own gay, swift Santa Fe streamliners. There'll be two of them—each of seven stainless steel cars, Diesel-electric drawn, and on 7 1/2 hour schedules.

On these trains, to enter regular service on or about *April 15th,* beauty and roomy comfort will feature the chair cars, with their rotating reclining seats; the combination lounges, parlor observation cars and Fred Harvey diners.

- The westbound streamliner, named The Kansas Cityan, will leave Chicago 9:00 A. M., arrive 4:30 P. M. The eastbound train, The Chicagoan, will leave Kansas City 2:10 P. M., arrive 9:35 P. M. This for finer, faster, daily Chicago-Kansas City service, with more convenient connections at either end!

The San Diegan

Now back to California, where, on or about March 15th, the shimmering new six-car, stainless steel SAN DIEGAN is to link Los Angeles and San Diego more closely.

The San Diegan will make two round trips daily, on a 2½-hour schedule, between these great Santa Fe terminal cities. Colorful and ultra-modern, with spacious chair cars, fine Fred Harvey meals in its bright lunch-tavern car, and an observation-parlor car, The San Diegan will bring new pleasure and speed to inter-city travel, and afford splendid connections with Santa Fe transcontinental trains in and out of Los Angeles.

Much new or improved equipment has been given to other long-established favorites among Santa Fe trains. For two years, also, as an essential part in this great program, Santa Fe has been improving roadbed, laying heavier steel, cutting grades and straightening curves. Those who ride with us in 1938 will enjoy the smooth, quiet sweep over Santa Fe rails.

Above: A portion of a 1938 pamphlet announcing the introduction of the new lightweight equipment reminds us that the ***San Diegans*** *were part of an extensive addition of equipment. Right: That idea is reinforced by this ticket envelope with slant-nosed E units going off to the horizon. In the thirties the sleek new streamlined equipment made quite a splash.*
Brian Norden Collection; Dennis Ryan Collection

Dining car service on the **San Diegans** *was in the Santa Fe tradition. Prices from this 1939 menu seem very attractive, but to put things in perspective, an average wage in 1939 was $100/month.* **Dennis Ryan Collection**

A la Carte

Prices shown on this menu are subject to 3% California Sales Tax

RELISHES

Queen Olives 20 — Gherkins 20 — Chow Chow 25

COLD DISHES

French Boneless Sardines 55 — Ham 50
Ox Tongue 55 — Boston Baked Beans with Brown Bread, Hot or Cold 30

SALADS

Lettuce, full portion 25; plate 15 — Potato 20
Chicken (white meat) 60 — Combination 30

POTATOES

Boiled 10 — Mashed 10 — Hashed Browned 15

SANDWICHES

Ham or Cheese 20 — Chicken 40 — Chicken Salad on Toast 40
Bacon, Lettuce and Tomato 30 — Tongue 25 — Club 55

BREAD, ETC.

Rye or Vienna Bread and Butter 10 — Boston Brown, Raisin or Whole Wheat 10
Dry or Buttered Toast 10 — Melba Toast 15 — Ry-Krisp 10
Shredded Wheat Biscuits with Cream 25 — Milk Toast 25

FRUITS AND PRESERVES

Orange, one 10 — Sliced Orange 15 — Apple, one 5
California Select Prunes 20 — Preserved Strawberries 20
Preserved Figs 25 — Orange Marmalade 20

CHEESE

American, with Water Crackers 20

BEVERAGES

Coffee, per pot 20; cup 10 — Sanka Coffee, per pot 20
Cocoa or Chocolate, Whipped Cream, per pot 20; cup 10 — Postum 15
Tea - Ceylon, Young Hyson, English Breakfast, Orange Pekoe, per pot 15
Milk, per bottle 10

Steward will gladly arrange for any special diet

An extra charge of Twenty-five cents each will be made for all meals served outside of Dining Car

SANTA FE DINING CAR SERVICE
FRED HARVEY

Table d'Hote Luncheons

Order by Number and Indicate Items Desired

NUMBER ONE—FIFTY CENTS

Filets of Halibut, Saute Anglaise
or
Spring Lamb Stew with Fresh String Beans
Potatoes, Persillade — Buttered Carrots, Vichy
Bread and Butter
Coffee — Tea — Milk

NUMBER TWO—SIXTY-FIVE CENTS

Chicken Croquettes with Sauce Supreme, June Peas
or
Pork Chop Saute Country Style, Candied Apple Slices
Mashed Potatoes — Chef's Special Salad
Bread and Butter
Vanilla Ice Cream or Layer Cake
Coffee — Tea — Milk

NUMBER THREE—EIGHTY CENTS

Consomme
Chicken a la King, Melba Toast
or
Grilled Lamb Chops
Mashed Potatoes — Fresh String Beans
Bread and Butter
Ice Cream with Cookies or Layer Cake
Coffee — Tea — Milk

Please Do Not Request Substitutions

The dining car menu cover at left is from 1942. Other services are represented by a lounge car menu (below) from 1969, and a promotional brochure for Custom Class (below, left), inaugurated in 1985.
Dennis Ryan Collection; Dick Stephenson Collection

Amtrak's Custom Class Service between San Diego and Los Angeles

Experience the Executive Prerogative:

Amtrak knows you want comfort and style when you travel between San Diego and Los Angeles . . . that's the relaxing reason for Custom Class Service.

Custom Class is our premium service for both the busy executive and the discriminating pleasure traveler. It's perfect for anyone who demands a more luxurious way of traveling without the hassles of crowded airports or sitting in rush hour traffic.

So, if you're traveling between San Diego and Los Angeles, you deserve to experience the executive prerogative: Amtrak's Custom Class Service.

Refreshments Santa Fe

Cocktails

Manhattan . . . . .95 Martini, Dry 95
Martini, Very Dry (**14 to 1**) English Gin - French Vermouth 1.00

Liquors and Beer

Canadian Whisky . . Ind. 1.00 Rum . . . . Ind. 90
Scotch Whisky . . . Ind. 1.00 Vodka . . . . Ind. 90
Gin . . . . Ind. 90 Brandy . . . . Ind. 90
Beer, Can . . . . .55 Ale, Can - Ballantine 65
Bourbon Whiskey, Bonded or Straight . . . . Ind. 1.00

Mixed Drinks

Drinks mixed with Ind. 5½ oz. can of Club Soda, Tonic Water,
Bitter Lemon or Ginger Ale . . . . 20c. extra
Snap-E-Tom, Tomato Juice, or Orange Juice . . . . 30c. extra

No extra charge for Highball or Old Fashioned made with water

Soft Drinks

Coca-Cola (12 oz. Can) . . .30 7 Up (12 oz. Can) 30
Lemonade (Made with Fresh Lemon Juice) . . . . Glass 50
Orangeade (Made with Freshly Squeezed Oranges) . . . . Glass 50

Cigars, Cigarettes, Playing Cards, Etc.

Cigars . . . . 10-15 Bromo Seltzer . . . . . . Ind. 15
Assorted Nuts . . . . .65 Alka Seltzer . . . . Ind. 15
Cigarettes (No Sales in Iowa) 50
Souvenir Playing Cards, Single Deck 1.25; Double Deck 2.50
Pinochle Playing Cards, Single Deck 1.00

Please remain seated while being served to avoid possible injuries.

Prices shown are subject to various occupation expense, school and sales taxes except as indicated on reverse side of this list.

For your protection, Liquor and cordials are served in original individual bottles which employees are required to open in your presence. The sale of liquor in individual bottles to be carried away is prohibited by law.

Sales of alcoholic beverages and cigarettes to persons under 21 is prohibited in all states.

No Bar Sales After 12:00 Midnight.

23-SD 6-69 5683

6

A San Diegan *Color Sampler*

OVER THE PAST 50 years the appearance of the *San Diegans* has changed considerably, as has much of the landscape they run over. In this selection of photos, we offer a varied look at the changing trains and changing times of the Surf Line. It is a colorful assortment which commands your attention.

Opposite page: Two walkers pause to observe the passage of **San Diegan** *No. 577 from the bluffs at Del Mar on August 6, 1988. Few beachgoers are in place this early in the morning. Right: A reminder of days gone by is this postcard scene of the San Diego depot complete with portico and a San Diego Electric Ry. PCC on the loop in front of the depot in the mid-forties. The portico was removed in 1954; that area is now a parking lot.* **Dick Stephenson; Dennis Ryan Collection**

4547—Santa Fe Station, San Diego, California

1B-H1011

Above: F3A No. 31 heads an A-B-B-A set on No. 72 out of Del Mar on November 13, 1955. Many things in this scene have changed since that time, as there has been considerable growth and construction in this quaint seaside village that is no longer on the main highway. Left: RDC car Nos. 191–192 round the curve into Del Mar on November 13, 1955, operating as train No. 83. Just two months later the cars were damaged in a tragic derailment at Redondo Junction. **Both, John E. Shaw**

Right: Long before industry and houses encroached on the area, Miramar was out in the country as compared with the city of San Diego. A southbound **San Diegan** *heads downgrade on May 12, 1957. Below: Whether known as Linda Vista or Miramar, this location at the top of Rose Canyon just north of San Diego still has significance. Miramar Hill is the most difficult grade on the Surf Line, previously requiring the use of helpers. In this scene, a* **San Diegan** *has just topped the hill, and heads into the last lap on its way to San Diego in March 1958.*

Both photos, John E. Shaw

Above: F3A No. 34 and three sisters are in charge of No. 77 at San Diego in the mid-fifties. Though some of the surroundings have changed, thousands of similar pictures have been taken over the years. Right: Alco PA No. 51 leads No. 73 as it slows to a stop at old San Clemente station, in July 1959. Unmanned, the neat little stucco depot did not have much time left; it was razed the next year. Trains then began stopping a mile south at the San Clemente pier (and they still do).
Jim Walker; Bob Kern

Left: This was a scene that was repeated often during the sixties, as PA No. 63L and a sister are at the San Diego depot on March 7, 1964. Below: In a timeless scene, No. 76 heads across Buena Vista Lagoon south of Oceanside in May 1968. The consist is very typical, and includes the original semi-lightweight car and a group of 3100-series coaches.

Jim Walker; Rick Peterson

Right: F7 No. 309 and three boosters lay over at Del Mar with a 22-car consist on September 7, 1968, the last day of racing for that season. The siding and wye were removed in 1972, and racing fans now must walk about a half mile from Del Mar station to the grandstands. For a long time heavyweights were the standard equipment for the Del Mar Race trains. Below: This October 1968 shot captures U30CG No. 404 backing No. 72 out of L.A. Union Station; U28CGs and U30CGs were used for a five-month period in late 1968 and early 1969. The equipment in the train is a mixture from four different orders.

John E. Shaw; Bob Kern

Above: Train No. 74 eases past Redondo Junction on September 1, 1969. It was on this curve that the RDCs derailed in January 1956. In the background, Santa Fe Alco switchers including an HH1000 look on. Right: The normally sleepy Fallbrook Branch became very busy on this day in November 1966, with not one, but two excursion trains operating to Fallbrook. One originated at Los Angeles, the other at National City. They meet here at Fallbrook Junction, just north of Oceanside, and officials and crews confer. The branch had once been part of the original California Southern Railway main line.
John E. Shaw; Dennis J. Kogan

Above: On May 1, 1971 (the first day of service for Amtrak), No. 77 speeds along near Del Mar Racetrack with a healthy consist in tow. Right: Heading north toward Los Angeles near Irvine in July 1971, the through cars for Seattle are on the rear of No. 98. The last car is Northern Pacific No. 364, a 10-roomette, six-bedroom car originally assigned to another through service: Seattle to Oakland on the ***Cascade.***

John E. Shaw; Jim Minor

Right: ***San Diegans*** *looked much the same, for a time, as they always had after Amtrak took over. Here at Sorrento F7A No. 309 leads two boosters handling No. 77 on its way back to Los Angeles on July 24, 1971. Below: In a scene that has changed considerably over the years, No. 74 meets No. 75 at the west end of Orange siding. The area is now built up with industrial buildings, and orange groves are only a memory.*

John E. Shaw; Cliff Prather

Left: In a scene that cannot be repeated today, ***Victoria*** *rests on the private car track at San Diego, while on the main line ex-SCL coach-observation No. 3345 graces the rear of No. 77 on August 19, 1973. Below: No. 70, powered by SDP40F No. 512 and E9B No. 452, blasts past Amtrak's 8th Street coach yard in Los Angeles in April 1975. Coming through the washer is the* ***Sunset Limited,*** *pulled by a Santa Fe CF7. The ex-troop kitchen cars to the left were used for storage.*
Both: Dick Stephenson

Right: From time to time, motive power failures necessitated the use of freight units. Here in June 1975, AT&SF GP35 No. 3442 leads E9B No. 451 with a northbound train near Tustin. Below: Where once there was no depot, now Anaheim Stadium station has been located. Seen here from the 57 Freeway (which was almost completed but not yet opened), No. 72 heads past the stadium behind E9 Nos. 416 and 451 on September 1, 1975.
Jim Minor; Dick Stephenson

Left: The last big-time steam operation on the Surf Line was not pulled by a Santa Fe engine, but by ex-Southern Pacific ***Daylight*** *GS4 No. 4449, seen here at Fullerton headed for Miramar on January 9, 1976, with the* ***American Freedom Train.*** *The train was also displayed at San Juan Capistrano. It then headed for points east after completing almost two months in the Golden State. Below: Freight plays a decreasingly important role on the Surf Line. This shot of a westbound freight at Valencia on January 24, 1976, serves as a reminder that agriculture has declined significantly along the Surf Line. The lead unit, GP35 No. 3442, is also seen on page 97 on a* ***San Diegan.***
Cliff Prather; Dick Stephenson

Right: Not a monster **San Diegan,** *this special train marked the arrival of Amfleet in Southern California on May 7, 1976. The SDP40F was used because it was equipped with automatic train stop (though the F40s had this added before entering service on Santa Fe trackage). Below: A stormy March 1978 day provides the backdrop for the* **El Camino** *as it heads south through Irvine. SDP40F No. 505 is doing the honors, which included providing steam to heat the cars.*

Dick Stephenson; Jim Minor

Backing out of Los Angeles Union Station, No. 72 is basking in the bright sun of a remarkable day on February 3, 1979. A large storm had blanketed the mountains around the city with a liberal coating of snow. On the rear of the train is private car **City of Cleveland** *(ex-Amtrak No. 3253, ex-Nickel Plate sleeper-lounge). Below: Heading north to Los Angeles, No. 773 glides through the orange groves of Rancho Capistrano and is about to cross Trabuco Creek, just north of San Juan Capistrano in January 1980. It has become difficult to find scenes such as this one, which is typical of the way the line used to look.*

Both: Dick Stephenson

Superliners have appeared only rarely on the Surf Line. This special was operated in conjunction with Family Days at San Diego on March 13–14, 1982. With an F40 on each end, the push-pull train operated to Miramar and return on an hourly schedule. The train is near Elvira in Rose Canyon, in an area which has recently been built up with condos (see page 109). Left: No. 772 heads south under threatening skies through Valencia on January 2, 1982. The old bean processing plant in the background has now been converted to a motel.
Dick Stephenson; Cliff Prather

Above: No large crowds were on hand to observe the Santa Fe Security Analysts' Special as it made its way north from San Diego past San Clemente State Beach on May 3, 1984. FP45 No. 5992 and two sisters handled this train with ease. Right: No. 772 zips along at Tustin, south of Santa Ana in July 1985. The tracks at right are used for freight car distribution to local industries. The hangar (originally used for blimps) in the background is an easily recognized landmark in the area.
David Busse; Jim Minor

Left: ***Cyrus K. Holliday*** *is on the rear of No. 576 as it pauses at Fullerton on December 7, 1985. Santa Fe GP9 No. 2285 is typical of the local road-switchers that tie up at the depot. Below: Certainly one of the most colorful and varied trains to operate on the Surf Line in recent times was the California Operation Lifesaver Special on April 23, 1987. Motive power included Santa Fe FP45 No. 5998, Union Pacific E9A No. 951, Southern Pacific SDP45 No. 3201 and Amtrak F40 No. 240. The train is seen near Cardiff on its southbound trip.* **Bill Volkmer; Jim Minor**

Top left: San Juan Capistrano depot has been a restaurant since 1975, but maintains its classic beauty. Top center: The Oceanside Intermodal Transportation Center features open space and airiness, as seen on January 19, 1988. Top right: Ceremonies were held at San Diego on October 26, 1987, to mark the start of the eighth daily train and push-pull service. Bottom left: Two F40s accelerate an 11-car No. 583 west out of Fullerton on August 30, 1987, into the sunset. Bottom right: Weekend-only No. 575 pauses at the Santa Ana Transportation Center on January 31, 1988 (Super Bowl Sunday).

Two photos, Dick Stephenson; Michael Blaszak; Cliff Prather; Dick Stephenson

Above: ***San Diegan*** *No. 577 heads north at Miramar on April 5, 1988, just after the Miramar Turn has been by to switch local industries. Below: The local, seen here the same day at Miramar, was down to running two or sometimes three days per week in 1988.*

Both: Michael Blaszak

Left: The pre-inaugural run of the Santa Barbara extension of ***San Diegan*** *service provided a daytime trip along the route. Here the train has arrived at Santa Barbara station on June 25, 1988. Regular service began the next morning. Below: The San Bernardino Subdivision represents big-time railroading, exemplified here in Santa Fe Springs with the eastbound* ***Desert Wind*** *running on the north track on July 19, 1988, behind F40 No. 234.*

Both: Dick Stephenson

Top left: Work on the rail replacement project was done at night, and here early in the morning of July 21, 1988, the rail gang is about to call it quits as they pass through Orange. Above: The narrow right-of-way in Santa Ana is emphasized by No. 580, as it heads south on August 13, 1988, in the "push" mode. The newly laid welded rail can be seen. Below: No. 570, about to meet No. 573, heads southbound into the siding at San Onofre on August 27, 1988. I-5 parallels the tracks to the right; the Pacific Ocean is to the left. **Michael Blaszak; two photos, Dick Stephenson**

Above: New houses bracket No. 783 as it heads north through Rose Canyon on its way toward Los Angeles and Santa Barbara on October 12, 1988. Right: A current view of the west side of the San Diego station from the parking lot where the coach yard and freight house used to be. On October 12, 1988, the Koll Center was under construction, due to be completed in July 1989.

Both: Dick Stephenson

BIBLIOGRAPHY

Santa Fe, The Railroad That Built an Empire, by James Marshall, Random House, 1945.

Railroads at War, by Skip Farrington, Coward-McCann, 1945.

Santa Fe's Diesel Fleet, by Joe McMillan, Chatham Publishing Co., 1975.

Rail Passenger Development Plan, 1988–1993 Fiscal Years, State of California, Department of Transportation, March 1988.

The San Diego depot tower is silhouetted against the dusk sky on October 12, 1988, a lasting symbol of Santa Fe's presence in San Diego. **Dick Stephenson**

Dispatcher, Railway Historical Society of San Diego, October 24, 1965 issue, edited by Eric B. Sanders; also various issues September 1965–October 1967.

Orange County Register, December 22, 1965.

Los Angeles Times, November 20, 1965.

California Public Utilities Commission, Decisions 68271 (November 24, 1964); 69511 (August 3, 1965); 69660 (September 8, 1965, denying rehearing).

Santa Fe Railway employees and public timetables, various dates between 1925 and 1988, author's collection.

Train orders, bulletins, timeslips and other miscellany from the late Dan C. Kurtz, now in author's collection.

The typeface used in this book is Times Roman

Typesetting: Roc-Pacific Typographics, Los Angeles

Color Separations, Image Assembly, and Printing: Walsworth Press Co., Marceline, Missouri

Book Design and Layout by Paul Hammond

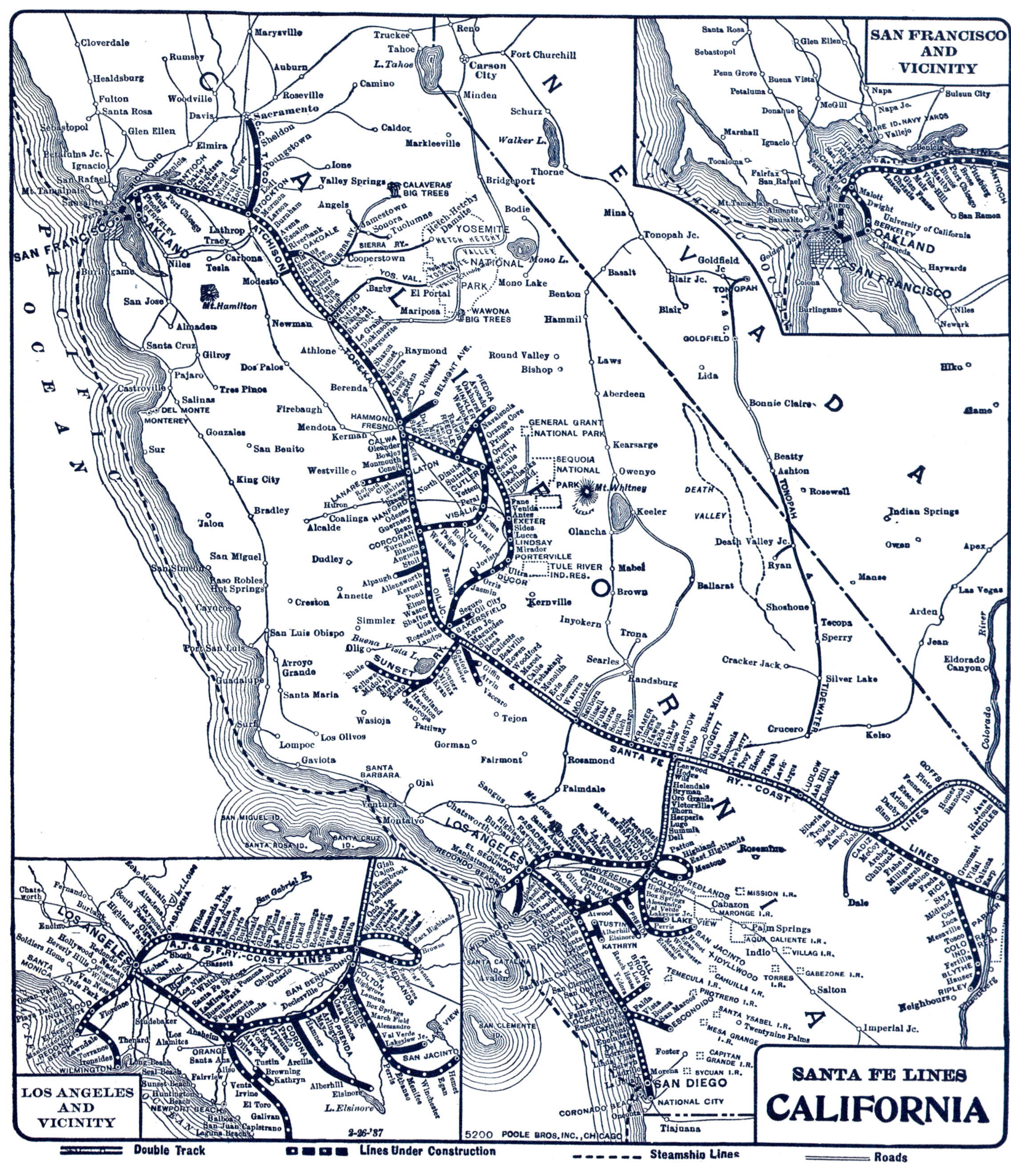

SANTA FE LINES
CALIFORNIA
SAN FRANCISCO AND VICINITY
LOS ANGELES AND VICINITY
PACIFIC OCEAN
CALIFORNIA
NEVADA
SANTA FE RY. - COAST LINES
A.T.& S.F.RY.-COAST LINES
ATCHISON
TOPEKA
SUNSET RY.
TIDEWATER
TONOPAH
YOSEMITE NATIONAL PARK
GENERAL GRANT NATIONAL PARK
SEQUOIA NATIONAL PARK
TULE RIVER IND. RES.
Mt. Whitney
Mt. Hamilton
CALAVERAS BIG TREES
WAWONA BIG TREES
Death Valley Jc.
DEATH VALLEY
L. Tahoe
Mono L.
Walker L.
Colorado River
SAN FRANCISCO
OAKLAND
BERKELEY
RICHMOND
STOCKTON
Sacramento
MERCED
FRESNO
HANFORD
VISALIA
BAKERSFIELD
MOJAVE
BARSTOW
NEEDLES
LOS ANGELES
PASADENA
SAN BERNARDINO
RIVERSIDE
REDLANDS
SAN DIEGO
NATIONAL CITY
Tijuana
SANTA BARBARA
Reno
Carson City
Goldfield
Las Vegas
SAN MIGUEL ID.
SANTA ROSA ID.
SANTA CRUZ ID.
SANTA CATALINA ID.
SAN CLEMENTE ID.
2-26-'37
5200 POOLE BROS. INC., CHICAGO
Double Track
Lines Under Construction
Steamship Lines
Roads